A National Police in America

"Is it Time for Change?"

Curtis B. Page, Jr., MA

A National Police in America
"Is it Time for Change?"

Curtis B. Page, Jr., MA

Every effort has been made to be accurate. The author assumes no responsibility or liability for errors made in this book. To report errors, please send e-mail to: contact@ NationalPolice.info

www.NationalPolice.info

ISBN: 978-0-9961857-1-4

Table of Contents

DEDICATION

This book is dedicated to the memory of my dearest mother, Mrs. Vergie Bell Page. Her life was tragically taken during a case of domestic violence. Mom's inspiration served as a beacon that guided my career from beginning to end. God bless Mom and God speed to the heavens

"Our task is not to fix the blame for the past, but to fix the course for the future" —**President John F. Kennedy**

PREFACE

This book offers an alternative to the law enforcement systems we currently have in the United States. It does not render a position upon which America must adopt going forward in the 21st century. The police forces have the most important job in our country and serves as the front line of defense for domestic public safety. Overall, they perform admirably in their duties and responsibilities.

As Americans, we have an obligation to provide law enforcement with the best tools available to keep the public safe. When compared against all other law enforcement systems around the world, our system is unmatched and quite frankly the best.

However, as was needed in America's early years, the founding fathers found it necessary to replace the Articles of Confederation with the Constitution in order to make our union more perfect.

Today, police forces in America are at a crossroad. This book examines the history of police forces in our country and ponders the future of policing. It may not be the solution to all problems inherent with public safety. However, the book does offer an alternative. This book presents what the government would need to do to implement a national force and ponder the benefits and drawbacks of a National Police Agency in America.

Our system is in need of cultural and structural reform to make it more perfect. Regardless of which path is chosen, the number one priority should be the safety of the American people. Public safety is a thankless and difficult task to master; but it can be mastered.

The research for this book was originally prepared as a class project while attending graduate studies at Webster University in San Diego, California. The book is based on interviews with everyday Americans, college students, public employees and officials of relevant agencies and institutions, direct observations, and a review of applicable documents.

The opinions, observations, and recommendations, therein, have been developed based on the best knowledge available to me. In addition, as appropriate, it has been discussed in draft with some of the officials who contributed to this study. Since the start of this project, one of the contributors, Union Parish Sheriff Robert "Bob" Buckley passed away quietly in 2014 after a battle with cancer.

—Curtis B. Page, Jr.

※

ABOUT THE AUTHOR

I was born and raised in Farmerville, Louisiana. I enlisted in the U. S. Navy two days after graduating high school in May 1979. My Navy career began as a deck seaman aboard USS Frank Cable (AS-40) in Seattle, Washington which culminated into a successful career in military police operations. I served for a short period of time as the ship's Legal Clerk and Legalman, a career field equivalent to civilian Paralegal Specialists.

My chosen career path steered me to the Navy's Military Police Corps (Navy Security Forces). During this time period, the

President Clinton & LCDR Curtis B. Page, Jr.

Navy implemented a modernization plan for its Security Forces. This included a transformation from Shore Patrol to a Navy Security Police Force operation, Physical Security to protect its assets, and Force Protection to protect its personnel. I also served in two civilian police agencies: Millington Police Department (Millington, Tennessee) and Kitsap County Sheriff's Office (Bremerton, Washington).

Over the next 25+ years, I advanced through the enlisted ranks to Chief Petty Officer and was commissioned an Ensign in October 1992. As a Limited Duty Officer (LDO) and Mustang, highlights of my career assignments included:

- Director of Navy Security Forces, Brig Officer, Physical Security Officer and Force Protection Officer, USS Abraham Lincoln (CVN-72)

- Assistant Director of Navy Security Forces, Naval Air Station, North Island, California

- Director of Navy Security Forces and Force Protection Officer, Naval Air Station, Jacksonville, Florida

- Director of Navy Security Forces and Force Protection Officer, Naval Air Station, Sigonella (Sicily)

- Director of Navy Security Forces, USS Nimitz (CVN-72)

Along the way, I participated in major planning programs and served on numerous committees responsible for shaping today's modern Navy Security Forces. In January 2005, I retired from the U. S. Navy at the rank of Lieutenant Commander and worked as an Adviser and Subject Matter Expert for Military Police Operations, Navy Security and Force Protection at Battelle Memorial Institute, a defense contractor headquartered in Columbus, Ohio. I have an Associate of Arts degree, Bachelors of Science degree in Criminal Justice Administration and a Master's degree in Business Organizational Security Management.

※

INTRODUCTION

Should the people of the United States of America (USA) consider a transformation of public safety to a centrally managed National Police Organization (NPO)? Can national government be trusted to organize, manage resources, and provide transformational leadership to local communities?

This book examines an alternative to the current police models in the USA to a national police that is organized, managed, and implemented by the federal government. Interviews, discussions, and meetings from a cross section of citizens and government officials found that the majority of America oppose a National Police Organization that would provide essential reactive law enforcement and proactive community oriented policing. There are both pros and cons to the concept of nationalizing police responsibilities.

※

CHAPTER 1 - HISTORY OF POLICE IN THE U.S.
Tracing History: Law Enforcement Yesterday, Today, and Tomorrow

Tracing U.S. Law Enforcement History

To help find the answer to the question of how a National Police Agency would work in the U.S., it is necessary to journey back to the origins of police in America. Like much of the American adversarial criminal justice system, this limited law enforcement model originated in England.

America's familiar law enforcement system, in which uniformed police officers respond to calls for help and plainclothes detectives investigate, was developed hundreds of years ago in England.

One of the early systems created was the Constable Watch System. This was a system of protection in early England in which citizens under the direction of a Constable, or Chief Peacekeeper were required to guard the city and pursue criminals as necessary. A Constable (which is still in existence today - Texas) was the peacekeeper in charge of protection in early English towns.

The Industrial Revolution brought a huge influx of people into London and along with them came increased poverty, public disorder, and crime. In 1829, Parliament created the London Metropolitan Police, a 1,000-member professional force. The London Police were organized according to military rank and structure. The main function of the police was to prevent crime by preventive patrol of the community.

U.S. Law Enforcement Yesterday

Settlers to the new American colonies brought with them the Constable-Watch system, which became common (although not necessarily effective) in cities. In many rural areas, a Sheriff and posse system was commonly used.

In 1844, New York City created the first paid, unified police force in the U.S. Other cities followed suit creating their own police departments. Often police departments were merely an organization of the existing day and night watch. It was not until after the Civil War that police forces routinely began to wear uniforms and carry nightsticks.

In the South, the earliest form of policing was the plantation slave patrols. Slave codes prohibited slaves from meetings, leaving the plantation without permission and learning to read and write.

In the American frontier, justice often meant vigilantism. Self-protection remains very popular in the South and West. As more immigrants poured into the U.S. and the nation's growth continued to expand, as well as the inability of some local Sheriffs and Constables to control crime, the states began to create their own law enforcement agencies. Texas officially created the Rangers in 1835. Pennsylvania established the first modern state law enforcement agency in 1905. By the 1930s, every state had some form of state law enforcement agency.

Until the 1920s, local political leaders maintained complete control over the police force. The political and police systems in many cities were corrupt. Jobs, politics, and law enforcement all depended on paying money to the right person.

Until the late 19th century, there were no qualifications required for law enforcement officers. Cincinnati was the first city to require qualifications of police officers. High moral character and foot speed were among the many new standards developed. It was not until the early 20th Century that reformers began advocating training and education for police officers. Reformers also aimed to remove the police from political influences.

Not so many years ago in rural America, most of the police officers were not educated and rarely attended a police academy for Peace Officer Standards and Training (POST) certification. They were hired based on their standing in the community and their relationship to the Chief of Police or the Parish/County Sheriff. The people living in small towns and rural counties like the idea of knowing individual officers and the Chief of Police or Sheriff. They believe, rightly or wrongly, that by knowing these individuals they might be able to influence them to their advantage in minor cases.

U.S. Law Enforcement Organization Today

The Federal Police possess full federal authority as given to them under U.S. Code (USC). Federal Law Enforcement Officers are authorized to enforce various laws at the federal level and under certain circumstances, empowered to enforce some state and local laws. Most of these agencies have both uniformed Police Officers and plain-clothes Special Agents.

The agencies have nationwide jurisdiction for enforcement of federal law. All federal agencies are limited by the USC to investigating only matters that are explicitly within the power of the federal government. However, federal investigative powers have become very broad in practice, especially since the passage of the USA Patriot Act (Uniting and Strengthening America by Providing Appropriate Tools Required to Intercept and Obstruct Terrorism Act of 2001).

The U.S. Department of Justice (DOJ) is the largest law enforcement agency and handles most law enforcement duties at the federal level. The most notable agencies are the FBI, DEA, BATF, U.S. Marshals Service, and Bureau of Prisons (BOP).

Current Federal Law Enforcement and Police Agency Structure

In an effort to maintain law and order and to maintain the peace and safety of the community, over 87,000 government law enforcement agencies have evolved over the course of US history.

The following chart outlines the 87,000+ governmental law enforcement agencies that exist today.

Governments in the U. S.

Type	Number	Remarks
Federal Democracy System: Legislative – Executive – Judicial Commander in Chief of U.S. Armed Forces	1	U.S. Federal Government Capitol – Washington, DC
State Sovereign Legislative/Executive/Judicial Commander in Chief of National Guard	50	U.S. Territories (American Samoa, Guam, Puerto Rico, U.S. Virgin Islands, Northern Mariana Islands, Guantanamo Bay, Cuba)
County / Parish	3,034	
Municipal (city, town, village)	19,429	
Indian Tribal Reservation	310	Population estimated at 2.5M
Township (some states Town)	16,504	
Special Purpose (utility, fire, police, library, etc.)	35,052	
TOTAL	**87,886**	

CHAPTER 2 - NATURE OF THE WORK

Police Officers Protect Lives and Properties

Organization and Resources

The U.S. has more police departments than any other nation in the world. Virtually every community has its own police force, creating a great disparity in the quality of American police personnel and service. Below is a framework of each police department model under the U.S. police systems of the police systems in America.

Law Enforcement Framework

Police officers and detectives protect lives and property. Law enforcement officers' duties depend on the size and type of their organizations. For example, police and detectives pursue and apprehend individuals who break the law and then issue citations or give warnings. A large proportion of their time is spent writing reports and maintaining records of incidents. Most police officers patrol their jurisdictions and investigate any suspicious activity that they notice. They also respond to calls from individuals. Detectives who often are called agents or special agents, perform investigative duties such as gathering facts and collecting evidence (DOL, 2011).

State and Local Law Enforcement

Uniformed Police Officers have general law enforcement duties. They maintain regular patrols and respond to calls for service. Much of their time is spent responding to calls and doing paperwork. They may direct traffic at the scene of an accident, investigate a burglary, or give first aid to an accident victim. In large police departments, officers usually are assigned to a specific type of duty (DOL, 2011).

Some agencies have special geographic jurisdictions and enforcement responsibilities. Public college and university police forces, public school district police and agencies serving transportation systems and facilities are examples. Most law enforcement workers in special agencies are uniformed officers.

Some police officers specialize in a particular field, such as chemical and microscopic analysis, training and firearms instruction or handwriting and fingerprint identification. Others work with special units such as horseback, bicycle, motorcycle or harbor patrol, canine corps, special weapons and tactics (SWAT), or emergency response teams. A few local and special law enforcement officers primarily perform jail-related duties or work in courts.

Sheriffs and Deputy Sheriffs enforce the law on the county level. Sheriffs usually are elected to their posts and perform duties similar to those of a local or county police chief. Sheriff departments tend to be relatively small, most having fewer than 50 sworn officers. Deputy Sheriffs have law enforcement duties similar to those of officers in urban police departments. Police and sheriff deputies who provide security in city and county courts are sometimes called ***bailiffs***.

State Police Officers, sometimes called ***State Troopers*** or ***Highway Patrol Officers***, arrest criminals statewide and patrol highways to enforce motor vehicle laws and regulations. State police officers often issue traffic citations to motorists. At the scene of accidents, they may direct traffic, give first aid and call for emergency equipment. They also write reports used to determine the cause of the accident.

State police officers frequently are called upon to render assistance to other law enforcement agencies, especially those in rural areas or small towns.

State Highway Patrol Officers operate in every state except Hawaii. Most full-time sworn personnel are uniformed officers who regularly patrol and respond to calls for service. Others work as investigators, perform court-related duties, or carry out administrative or other assignments.

Detectives are plainclothes investigators who gather facts and collect evidence for criminal cases. Some are assigned to inter-agency task forces to combat specific types of crime. They conduct interviews, examine records, observe the activities of suspects and participate in raids or arrests. Detectives usually specialize in investigating one type of violation, such as homicide or fraud. They are assigned cases on a rotating basis and work on them until an arrest and conviction is made or until the case is dropped.

Fish and Game Wardens enforce fishing, hunting, and boating laws. They patrol hunting and fishing areas, conduct search and rescue operations, investigate complaints and accidents, and aid in prosecuting court cases.

Federal Law Enforcement

Federal Bureau of Investigation (FBI) Agents are the government's principle investigators, responsible for investigating violations of more than 200 categories of federal law and conducting sensitive national security investigations.

Agents may conduct surveillance, monitor court-authorized wiretaps, examine business records, investigate white-collar crime, or participate in sensitive undercover assignments.

The FBI investigates a wide range of criminal activity which includes organized crime, public corruption, financial crime, bank robbery, kidnapping, terrorism, espionage, drug trafficking, and cybercrime (DOL, 2011).

There are many other federal agencies that enforce particular types of laws. *U.S. Drug Enforcement Administration (DEA) Agents* enforce laws and regulations relating to illegal drugs. U.S. Marshals and Deputy Marshals provide security for the federal courts and ensure the effective operation of the judicial system. *Bureau of Alcohol, Tobacco, Firearms, and Explosives Agents* enforce and investigate violations of federal firearms and explosives laws, as well as federal alcohol and tobacco tax regulations. The *U.S. Department of State Bureau of Diplomatic Security Special Agents* are engaged in the battle against terrorism.

The *Department of Homeland Security* also employs numerous law enforcement officers within several different agencies, including Customs and Border Protection, Immigration and Customs Enforcement, and the U.S. Secret Service. *U.S. Border Patrol Agents* protect more than 8,000 miles of international land and water boundaries.

Immigration Inspectors interview and examine people seeking entry into the United States and its territories. *Customs Inspectors* enforce laws governing imports and exports by inspecting cargo, baggage and articles worn or carried by people, vessels, vehicles, trains, and aircraft entering or leaving the United States.

Federal Air Marshals provide air security by guarding against attacks targeting U.S. aircrafts, passengers, and crews. *U.S. Secret Service Special Agents* and *U.S. Secret Service Uniformed Officers* protect the President, the Vice President, their immediate families, and other public officials. Secret service special agents also investigate counterfeiting, forgery of government checks or bonds, and fraudulent use of credit cards.

Other federal agencies employ police and special agents with sworn arrest powers and the authority to carry firearms. These agencies include the **Postal Service**, the **Bureau of Indian Affairs Office of Law Enforcement**, the **Forest Service** and the **National Park Service**.

WORK ENVIRONMENT

Police and detective work can be very dangerous and stressful. Police officers and detectives have one of the highest rates of on-the-job injury and illness. In addition to the obvious dangers of confrontations with criminals, police officers and detectives need to be constantly alert and ready to deal appropriately with a number of other threatening situations. Many law enforcement officers witness death and suffering resulting from accidents and criminal behavior. A career in law enforcement may take a toll on their private lives.

Uniformed officers, detectives, agents, and inspectors usually are scheduled to work 40-hour weeks, but paid overtime is common. Shift work is necessary because protection must be provided around the clock. Junior officers frequently work weekends, holidays, and nights. Police officers and detectives are required to work whenever they are needed and may work long hours during investigations. Officers in most jurisdictions, whether on or off duty, are expected to be armed and to exercise their authority when necessary.

The jobs of some federal agents such as U.S. Secret Service and DEA special agents require extensive travel, often on very short notice. These agents may relocate a number of times over the course of their careers. Some special agents such as those in the U.S. Border Patrol may work outdoors in rugged terrain and in all kinds of weather.

TRAINING, OTHER QUALIFICATIONS, and ADVANCEMENT

Education requirements range from a high school diploma to a college degree or higher. Most police and detectives learn much of what they need to know on the job, often in their agency's training academy. Civil service regulations govern the appointment of police and detectives in most states, large municipalities, and special police agencies, as well as in many smaller jurisdictions. Candidates must be U.S. citizens, usually at least 21 years old and meet rigorous physical and personal qualifications.

EDUCATION and TRAINING

Applicants usually must have at least a high school education and some departments require 1 or 2 years of college coursework and in some cases a college degree. Physical education classes and participation in sports are also helpful in developing the competitiveness, stamina, and agility needed for many law enforcement positions. Knowledge of a foreign language is an asset in many federal agencies and urban departments.

State and Local Agencies encourage applicants to take courses or training related to law enforcement subjects after high school. Many entry-level applicants for police jobs have completed some formal post-secondary education and a significant number are college graduates. Many junior colleges, colleges, and universities offer programs in law enforcement or administration of justice. Many agencies pay all or part of the tuition for officers to work toward degrees in criminal justice, police science, administration of justice, or public administration. Higher salaries are paid to those earning one of these degrees.

Before their first assignments, officers usually go through a period of training. In state and large local police departments, recruits get training in their agency's police academy, often for 12 to 14 weeks. In small agencies, recruits often attend a regional or state academy. Training includes classroom instruction in constitutional law and civil rights, state laws and local ordinances, and accident investigation.

Fish and Game Wardens also must meet specific requirements. Most states require at least two years of college study. Once hired, fish and game wardens attend a training academy lasting from three to 12 months, sometimes followed by further training in the field.

Federal Agencies require a bachelor's degree, related work experience, or a combination of the two. Federal law enforcement agents undergo extensive training, usually at the United States Marine Corps (USMC) base in Quantico, Virginia or the Federal Law Enforcement Training Center (FLETC) in Glynco, Georgia.

To be considered for appointment as an FBI Agent, an applicant must be a college graduate and have at least three years of professional work experience or must have an advanced degree plus two years of professional work experience. An applicant who meets these criteria also must have one of the following: a college major in accounting, electrical engineering, information technology or computer science, fluency in a foreign language, a degree from an accredited law school, or three years of related full-time work experience. All new FBI agents undergo 18 weeks of training at the FBI Academy at USMC base in Quantico, Virginia.

OTHER QUALIFICATIONS

Civil service regulations govern the appointment of police and detectives in most states, large municipalities, special police agencies, and in many small jurisdictions. Candidates must be U.S. citizens, usually must be at least 21 years old, and must meet rigorous physical and personal qualifications. Physical examinations for entry into law enforcement often include tests of vision, hearing, strength, and agility. Eligibility for appointment usually depends on one's performance in competitive written examinations and previous education and experience.

Candidates should enjoy working with people and meeting the public. Personal characteristics such as honesty, sound judgment, integrity, and a sense of responsibility are especially important in law enforcement. Candidates are interviewed by senior officers and their character traits and backgrounds are investigated. A history of domestic violence may disqualify a candidate. In some agencies, candidates are interviewed by a psychiatrist or a psychologist or given a personality test. Most applicants are subjected to lie detector examinations or drug testing. Some agencies subject sworn personnel to random drug testing as a condition of continuing employment.

Although similar in nature, the requirements for federal agents are generally more stringent and the background checks are more thorough. There are polygraph tests as well as interviews with references. Jobs that require security clearances have additional requirements.

Federal agents often are on the General Services (GS) pay scale. Most begin at the GS-5 or GS-7 level. As agents meet time-in-grade and knowledge and skills requirements, they move up the GS scale. Promotions at and above GS-13 are most often managerial positions. Many agencies hire internally for these supervisory positions. A few agents may be able to enter the Senior Executive Series (SES) ranks of upper management.

EMPLOYMENT

Police and detectives held about 883,600 jobs in 2008. About 79 percent were employed by local governments. State police agencies employed about 11 percent. Various federal agencies employ police and detectives (DOL, 2011).

According to the U.S. Bureau of Justice Statistics, police and detectives employed by local governments worked primarily in cities with more than 25,000 inhabitants. Some cities have very large police forces while thousands of small communities employ fewer than 25 officers each (DOL, 2011).

EARNINGS

Police and sheriff's patrol officers had median annual wages of $51,410 in May 2008. The middle 50 percent earned between $38,850 and $64,940. The lowest 10 percent earned less than $30,070 and the highest 10 percent earned more than $79,680. Median annual wages were $46,620 in federal government, $57,270 in state government, $51,020 in local government and $43,350 in educational services (DOL, 2011).

In May 2008, median annual wages of detectives and criminal investigators were $60,910. The middle 50 percent earned between $45,930 and $81,490. The lowest 10 percent earned less than $36,500 and the highest 10 percent earned more than $97,870. Median annual wages were $73,170 in federal government, $53,910 in state government and $55,930 in local government.

Federal law provides special salary rates to federal employees who serve in law enforcement. Additionally, federal special agents and inspectors receive law enforcement availability pay (LEAP) - equal to 25 percent of the agent's grade and step - awarded because of the large amount of overtime that these agents are expected to work. Salaries were slightly higher in selected areas where the prevailing local pay level was higher.

Total earnings for local, state and special police and detectives frequently exceed the stated salary because of payments for overtime, which can be significant. According to the International City – County Management Association's Annual Police and Fire Personnel, Salaries, and Expenditures Survey, average salaries for sworn full-time positions in 2008 were as follows:

Position	Minimum salary	Maximum Salary w/o Longevity
Police Chief	$90,570	$113,930
Deputy Police Chief	74,834	96,209
Police Captain	72,761	91,178
Police Lieutenant	65,688	79,268
Police Sergeant	58,739	70,349
Police Corporal	49,421	61,173

In addition to the common benefits - paid vacation, sick leave, and medical and life insurance - most police and sheriff departments provide officers with special allowances for uniforms. Many police officers retire at half-pay after 20 years of service; others often are eligible to retire with 30 or fewer years of service.

Corrections Framework

The jail population changes constantly; as some prisoners are released some are convicted and transferred to prison and new offenders are arrested and enter the system.

Correctional officers in local jails admit and process about 13 million people a year with nearly 800,000 offenders in jail at any given time. Correctional officers in state and federal prisons watch over the approximately 1.6 million offenders who are incarcerated there at any given time.

Typically, offenders serving time at county jails are sentenced to a year or less. Those serving a year or more are usually housed in state or federal prisons.

Correctional Officers

Correctional officers, also known as detention officers, when they work in pretrial detention facilities, are responsible for overseeing individuals who have been arrested and are awaiting trial or who have been convicted of a crime and sentenced to serve time in a jail, reformatory or penitentiary (DOL, 2011).

Correctional officers maintain security and inmate accountability to prevent disturbances, assaults, and escapes. Officers have no law enforcement responsibilities outside of the institution where they work (DOL, 2011).

Bailiffs, also known as Marshals or Court Officers, are law enforcement officers who maintain safety and order in courtrooms. Their duties, which vary by location, include enforcing courtroom rules, assisting judges, guarding juries from outside contact, delivering court documents and providing general security for courthouses.

WORK ENVIRONMENT

Working in a correctional institution can be stressful and hazardous. Every year correctional officers are injured in confrontations with inmates. Correctional officers and jailers have one of the highest rates of nonfatal on-the-job injuries. First-line supervisors/managers of correctional officers also face the risk of work-related injury. Correctional officers may work indoors or outdoors. Some correctional institutions are well lighted, temperature controlled and ventilated, but others are old, overcrowded, hot and noisy (DOL, 2011).

TRAINING, OTHER QUALIFICATIONS, and ADVANCEMENT

Correctional officers go through a training academy and then are assigned to a facility where they learn most of what they need to know for their work through on-the-job training. Qualifications vary by agency, but all agencies require a high school diploma or equivalent. Others require some college education or full-time work experience. Military experience is often seen as a plus for corrections employment.

EDUCATION and TRAINING

A high school diploma or graduation equivalency degree is required by all employers. The Federal Bureau of

Prisons (BOP) requires entry-level correctional officers to have at least a bachelor's degree, 3 years of full-time experience in a field providing counseling, assistance or supervision to individuals, or a combination of the two. Some state and local corrections agencies require some college credits, but law enforcement or military experience may be substituted to fulfill this requirement.

Academy trainees generally receive instruction in a number of subjects, including institutional policies, regulations and operations, as well as custody and security procedures. New federal correctional officers must undergo 200 hours of formal training within the first year of employment. They also must complete 120 hours of specialized training at BOP residential training center at FLETC within 60 days of their appointment. Experienced officers receive annual in-service training to keep abreast of new developments and procedures.

OTHER QUALIFICATIONS

All institutions require correctional officers to be at least 18 to 21 years of age, be a U.S. citizen or permanent resident and have no felony convictions. New applicants for federal corrections positions must be appointed before they are 37 years old. Some institutions require previous experience in law enforcement or the military. College credits can be substituted to fulfill this requirement. Others require a record of previous job stability, usually accomplished through two years of work experience, which need not be related to corrections or law enforcement.

EMPLOYMENT

Correctional officers and jailers held about 454,500 jobs in 2008, while first-line supervisors and managers of correctional officers held about 43,500 jobs. An additional 20,200 workers were employed as bailiffs. The vast majority of correctional officers and jailers and their supervisors were employed by state and local government in correctional institutions such as prisons, prison camps, and youth correctional facilities (DOL, 2011).

EARNINGS

Median annual wages of correctional officers and jailers were $38,380 in May 2008. The middle 50 percent earned between $29,660 and $51,000. The lowest 10 percent earned less than $25,300 and the highest 10 percent earned more than $64,110. Median annual wages in the public sector were $50,830 in the Federal Government, $38,850 in State government and $37,510 in local government. In the facilities support services industry, where the relatively small number of officers employed by privately operated prisons is classified, median annual wages were $28,790.

※

CHAPTER 3 - AMERICA READY FOR A CHANGE?

Is America Prepared for a National Police Force Patrolling Local Communities?

Today, in the wake of many events rising to a national crisis, the action words "merger" and "consolidation" offer hope for many, but devastation for others. Some of these national events will be addressed in more details later in this book. If merger and consolidation offer hope and could streamline how business is conducted; why would anyone object to such efficiency?

The Arguments

The Case "Against" a National Police Organization

Asking or allowing the federal government to intervene in local matters reduces the sovereign power of state and local governments. Such an agency is contrary to the Founders' design of the current form of government. Other roadblocks and concerns may include:

- Potential for insensitivity to local communities and their immediate public safety issues

- Potential for insensitivity to civil liberties

- Huge and unmanageable bureaucracy

- Potential for abuse of power

- Difficulty in checking uniformity, spending, and compliance

- No foundational check and balance system (e.g., local oversight and accountability)

- Potential loss of local non-enforcement services. (Many departments have officers who perform duties that are not appropriately classified as

police functions. Consolidation programs
commonly result in the discontinuation of such
services by the officers.)

Consolidation studies have shown that most leaders of
average to medium-sized police departments in the U.S. are
content with the operation of their departments, the services
provided, and the quality of the personnel they employ. The
same is true of the police officers employed within the
agencies. From their viewpoint, there is no reason to
consolidate their departments into a nationalized or even a
regional force locally or within the individual states.

Consolidation would bring uncertainty to the status of their
employment and the nature of their jobs. Understandably,
many of these officers and officials would argue against any
effort to consolidate their department with a new construct
(national) or consolidate with other police agencies in the
region. While these arguments are self-serving and perhaps
not in the interest of a more professional police service, they
are a legitimate expression of the fear of change and the need
to preserve the status quo.

The cost to the taxpayers to maintain a small police
department is relatively modest and is certainly less than the
cost of supporting a larger national force. The fact that a
national or regional force would be able to offer more service
and protection is rejected by the counter argument that these
communities do not need or require additional protection or
services.

Senator Diane Feinstein

"Efforts to prevent and address domestic crime have traditionally been the responsibility of state and local governments, with the federal government playing a supportive role. As crime rates increased throughout the 1960s, 1970s, and 1980s, the federal government became increasingly involved in anti-crime efforts. This was accomplished primarily through grant programs to encourage and assist states and communities in their efforts to control crime, and through expanding the number of offenses that could be prosecuted in federal courts. Completely replacing state and local law enforcement would be very controversial. To date, no legislation to do this has been introduced."
-**Senator Diane Feinstein**

UNSUCCESSFUL CONSOLIDATION STORIES

Case Study – Waterford Police Department Dissolution

In 2004, public officials in Waterford, New York, a small town of 8,515 residents attempted to dissolve its local police department and enter into a cooperative agreement with the Saratoga County Sheriff for police services. Cooperative agreements between municipalities generally are not easy to achieve. In Waterford, this was especially true if the agreement abridges the control of one of the jurisdictions or addresses quality of life factors, such as school options or public safety.

The initiative failed because it did not have the support of local law enforcement and more importantly, the citizens of Waterford. Observers in the Waterford area attributed the failure primarily because it threatened local control. Experts tend to agree that existing police departments are essentially unassailable given public resistance to dissolving them. This initiative grew into heated, confrontational, and disastrous public dissatisfaction.

The reasons for the rejection of the proposal surfaced in interviews and public documents. Isolating and clustering these factors helped deconstruct the prevailing sense that resistance to changes in policing was simply a knee-jerk reaction to threats to local control. Analysis suggests that there were five factors connected to rejection of the referendum in the Waterford case:

- The proposed arrangement failed to offer residents a credible substitute for the perceived system of local accountability and voice in matters of public security.

- The proposed arrangement failed to offer residents a credible substitute for the perceived law enforcement philosophy in place.

- The proposal did not address any compelling problems with public security or local finances for the majority of residents.

- The process was closed up to the point that the proposal was outlined.

- Opponents, particularly the policing community, responded aggressively to the proposal effectively using emotional arguments and tactics to thwart a fiscally sound proposal.

The people of Waterford had a perception of the law enforcement bargain (the approach and practices in use) they believed existed and resisted changes or substitutions that did not preserve the patterns, protections, and limits placed around security activities. In Waterford, the proposal addressed the structures of patrol and coverage, but did not deal with the residents' idea of policing. As such, the public did not trust that the public safety alternative provided by the Saratoga County Sheriff was a credible substitution. The public needed to know how oversight of policing services will occur and how the provider will be held accountable (UOA, 2007).

Case Study – City of Sparks, Nevada

Sparks, Nevada rejected calls for consolidating police services within their county even though they are less than 500 miles away from one of the nation's most successful police consolidation success story. According to the citizens and public officials, "bigger is not always better". The opponents of consolidation counter that greater fragmentation of local governments and increased competition between them will promote reductions in service costs, increased public access, and greater political accountability.

The superior fiscal performance of governments in a fragmented system comes from the effects of inter-jurisdictional competition and from their ability to choose from a variety of service arrangements of various scales (ACIR, 1992).

Where contracting out is an option, even the smallest cities can take advantage of economies of scale, where they exist through contracts with outside (public or private) service providers. The opponents also charged that consolidation undermines community identity and reduces political accessibility and accountability by further removing elected representatives from their constituents. They argued that decentralized structures are inherently more democratic for the simple reason that they are closer to the people.

The most popular argument advanced by the pro-consolidation advocates was that of cost savings through "economies of scale". The assumption was that consolidation would result in cost savings by reducing duplication and the number of employees.

However, many of the case studies on consolidations in both the U.S. and Canada over the last 20 years have failed to find significant economies of scale for most municipal services. The findings from these and other studies have shown that costs for many services actually increase following large municipal consolidations.

There are many studies available against consolidation. For example, consolidated city services that are labor-intensive and must be replicated from one neighborhood to the next (e.g., police patrols, fire stations, and parks) often do not achieve economies of scale and may end up costing the same or even more. When local governments consolidate, the wages of the consolidated government's employees usually increase to the level of the highest-paid comparable employees.

A similar "averaging up" phenomenon occurs with service levels and standards for equipment and facilities which also tends to rise to the highest level among the consolidating organizations. As a result, many of the cost savings that may be achieved by streamlining services and staff are often offset by the absence of scale economies and the averaging up of wages and service standards. In contrast, the evidence from various studies has led many researchers to conclude that the least expensive local governments are found in complex systems of small and medium-sized municipalities that both compete and cooperate with one another (Bish, 2001).

In September 2011, Public Broadcasting Station (PBS) Frontline broadcast the results of a two year investigative project from the Washington Post on national security by investigative journalists; Dana Priest and William Arkin. The program, Top Secret America, unveiled a massive national security buildup in the U.S. after the September 11, 2001 attacks (Washington Post, 2011).

Priest and Arkin discovered that when it comes to national security, all too often, no expense is spared and few questions are asked resulting in an enterprise so massive that nobody in government has a full understanding of its' enormity.

In the program, Priest and Arkin described the national security landscape as an alternative geography of America, a "Top Secret America", hidden from public view and lacking in thorough oversight. After 10 years of unprecedented spending and growth, the result was that the system put in place to keep the U.S. safe was so massive that its effectiveness was impossible to determine.

The investigation's other findings included:

- Some 1,271 government organizations and 1,931 private companies work on programs related to counter-terrorism, homeland security, and intelligence in about 10,000 locations across the U.S.

- An estimated 854,000 people, nearly 1.5 times as many people who live in the District of Columbia, hold top secret security clearances.

- In the District of Columbia and the surrounding area, 33 building complexes for top secret intelligence work are under construction or have been built since September 2001. Together they occupy the equivalent of almost three Pentagons or twenty-two U.S. Capitol buildings which is approximately 17 million square feet of space.

Many studies on consolidating police agencies have found overwhelming evidence that most citizens do not want to relinquish control of important local powers to a large consolidated government entity. In this case, a central government police agency would have near limitless powers.

A consolidated government means, fundamentally, that fewer people will be making decisions for a larger number of people. Many individuals would lose more power or control than they would gain.

FBI Special Agent in Charge Keith Slotter, San Diego Field Office

Agent Keith Slotter

Supervisory Special Agent Keith Slotter, Special Agent in Charge (SAC) of the FBI San Diego Field Office, opposes creation of a National Police Force. He believes a national police would weaken rather than strengthen America's law enforcement and intelligence gathering capabilities. (Appendix A).

U.S. Representative Duncan Hunter, 52nd District CA

Representative Duncan Hunter

U.S. Representative Duncan Hunter (R) joined in the discussion on a national police agency in the U.S. Congressman Hunter is an Iraq War veteran and a Reserve Marine Corps Captain. He opposes a National Police Force and believes by adding a national police organization to the list of existing law enforcement agencies nationwide would likely serve to disrupt the relationship between the agencies and would be counter-productive to the constitution's perspective for policing. He also believes the new organization would deeply challenge the 10th amendment. (Appendix A)

The Case "For" a National Police Organization

According to government service representatives and academic law experts, consolidating departments is cost effective, gives smaller departments' access to previously unavailable resources, and could decrease duplicate efforts performed by different departments.

A larger pool of officers could provide consistent enforcement, improved training, and wider distribution. Centralized record keeping, laboratories, and services are all possible through consolidation.

Accountability and management could also improve through effective consolidation planning.

Even with this cost savings, the majority of citizens and municipal governments prefer to maintain local control of law enforcement services and cite a fear of losing the "personalized" service provided by local law enforcement.

Consolidating departments would create the opportunity to act more decisively and more strategically to achieve important new benefits. This probably could not be achieved without consolidation.

The benefits of consolidation include:

- Makes it possible to develop, articulate, implement, and measure the results of a single comprehensive public safety strategy

- Having one plan promotes efficiency by eliminating the need to coordinate multiple plans

- Makes it possible for elected officials and law enforcement leaders to articulate a clear vision to the public vice defending differences in departments

- Integrates enforcement priorities with correctional resources and policies

- Correctional resources can be programmed to better support enforcement goals and activities

- Strategy can be supported and implemented through a single budget

- Consolidation will reduce the variation and improve public understanding and support

- Accountable to a single set of core performance measures

- Responsibility for results is more clearly in the hands of the department head and the governing body

- Reduces or eliminates jurisdictional questions and obstacles

- Opportunities to contain management and supervision costs over the long term by carefully managing attrition

CONSOLIDATION SUCCESS STORIES

The City of Las Vegas and Clark County, Nevada

In 1973, the five police agencies in Clark County (Clark County Sheriff's Department, City of Las Vegas Police Department, City of North Las Vegas Police Department, City of Henderson Police Department, and Boulder City Police Department) were consolidated into the Las Vegas Metropolitan Police Department (LVMPD).

Consolidation of the agencies had been studied several years prior to 1973. The study centered on areas that might prove feasible for consolidation including records, criminalistics, detention, and communications. The Committee performing the study concluded that full consolidation of the five agencies was the most practical solution, instead of a limited consolidation of one or more of the selected functional areas.

The consolidation was finalized by Nevada Senate Bill 340 (July 1, 1973). In effect, the new Las Vegas Metropolitan Police Department was headed by the elected county Sheriff (it was believed that an elected head would have more freedom from political pressure and would be more answerable directly to the public). Senate Bill 340 also provided for a police commission and designated funding sources. The new department retained responsibility of the operation of county jails. The consolidation costs included:

- Short-term commitments that could not be canceled (e.g. previous fleet purchase bids resulting in the need to repaint new cars)
- New uniforms
- Standardization of weapons

- Salary adjustments and benefits package modifications

According to officials in Las Vegas, the consolidation did not initially save money. However, the consolidation has saved a substantial amount of money over time. It has also improved overall efficiency, eliminated duplication of fixed resources, increased purchasing power, and increased teamwork (LVMPD 2011).

Los Angeles County, California

Over the last several years, the Los Angeles County Sheriff's Office (LACSO) has absorbed several other agencies including the LA County Transit Police, the Hawaiian Gardens Police Department, the Bell Gardens Police Department, and the LA Community College Police Department.

Discussions with personnel from LACSO indicates that in the case of each agency absorbed, the agency's budget has decreased by approximately 30%. Additionally, personnel from the absorbed agency have received a pay increase. Some other aspects of savings include background checks and physicals.

LACSO has seen a direct benefit to its recruits by having combined jail and policing duties. The sheriff's office is able to provide officers with experience in the county jail prior to placing them on regular patrol. This has resulted in a much shorter on-the-job learning curve for new officers. This has also reduced total costs by ensuring that personnel who undergo training at the Academy do not subsequently leave the force when presented with the actualities of the job. Furthermore, they generally become better officers, and overall, the officers are more effective (LACSO 2011).

Nashville, Tennessee Metropolitan Police Department

Nashville is a consolidated city-county government consisting seven smaller municipalities organized into a two-tier system. The population of Nashville-Davidson County stood at 626,144 as of 2008, according to US Census Bureau estimates; making it the second most populous city in the state behind Memphis. However, the 2009 population of the entire 13-county Nashville Metropolitan Statistical Area was 1,582,264; making it the largest metropolitan area in the state. The 2009 population of the combined Nashville-Davidson-Murfreesboro-Columbia statistical area was estimated at 1,666,566.

The City of Nashville and Davidson County merged in 1963 as a way for Nashville to combat the problems of urban sprawl. The combined entity is officially known as "the Metropolitan Government of Nashville and Davidson County" and is popularly known as "Metro Nashville" or simply "Metro". It offers services such as police, fire, electricity, and water and sewage treatment.

When the Metro government was formed in 1963, the government was split into two service districts; the urban services district and the general services district. The urban services district encompasses the 1963 boundaries of the former City of Nashville and the general services district includes the remainder of Davidson County.

There are seven smaller municipalities within the consolidated city-county: Belle Meade, Berry Hill, Forest Hills, Lakewood, Oak Hill, Goodlettsville (partially), and Ridgetop (partially). These municipalities use a two-tier system of government, with the smaller municipality typically providing police services and the Metro Nashville government providing most other services.

Nashville Metropolitan Police Department (NMPD) is the primary provider of law enforcement services for Metropolitan Nashville and Davidson County. NMPD covers a total area of 526 square miles that encompasses high density urban locations and rural areas.

The department comprises of over 1900 personnel, including over 1300 full-time sworn officers with an annual budget of $139,245,000. The department is configured in a decentralized format, providing its Precinct Commanders with control of their own resources to address issues and crime in their areas.

The department is divided into six precincts: North, South, East, West, Central, and Hermitage. A precinct is designed similarly to a medium-sized police department which includes uniformed patrol, plainclothes detectives, and other specialties (NMPD, 2010).

Why a National Police Agency?

Based on research, surveys, and field interviews, a large segment of Americans, particularly mid-westerners, would be suspicious of the federal government assuming control over the local police. Suspicions would arise because of what some describe as repeated demonstrations of distrust, insensitivity to constitutional guarantees, and the question of whether the government could effectively execute this task.

During the research for this book, field interviews were conducted with approximately 125 students who were attending various colleges and universities in the San Diego metropolitan area. Most of them being from the mid-west *(Illinois, Iowa, Kansas, Missouri, Nebraska, South Dakota, North Dakota and Wisconsin)* and the rust belt *(Indiana, Ohio, Michigan, New York, Pennsylvania and West Virginia).*

The breakdown consisted of 75 males which included 25 Caucasians, 15 African-Americans, 20 Hispanics, 10 Native American Indians, and 5 Asian-Americans; and 50 females which included 27 Caucasians, 10 Hispanics, 8 Asian-Americans, and 5 African-Americans.

Only about 15% of the students interviewed favored a National Police Agency run by the federal government, while 75% opposed a National Police Agency, and 10% had no opinion at all. The majority of the students had a rather harsh opinion of the federal government. This group also believed the federal government had already exceeded its constitutional powers, citing the abundance of federal law enforcement agencies already in place. However, most of the students were not very familiar with or had never read the 10th amendment.

The harshest opposition came from the mid-westerners who fiercely opposed any plan of the federal government replacing local and state police. 7 out of every 10 instances, the students cited three events for their distrust of the federal government. These were: the government's handling of the Ruby Ridge Incident, the government's handling of the Waco Siege, and Immigrations and Border Security – Ineffective Border Security.

Ruby Ridge

The government's handling of the Ruby Ridge Incident (August 22, 1992) took place on a remote ridge in northern Idaho. A week long standoff between white supremacist, Randy Weaver, and federal agents ended in a shootout in which an FBI Hostage Rescue Team sniper, Lon Horiuchi, shot and killed Weaver's wife, Vicki. The siege began a week earlier when U.S. Marshals tried to arrest Weaver for failing to appear in court on weapons charges. At that time, a gun battle erupted between the Marshals and the Weavers, resulting in the deaths of Weaver's 14 year old son Samuel and Deputy U.S. Marshal Bill Degan.

Waco

In the government's handling of the Waco Siege (February 28, 1993), a force of seventy-six agents from the BATF tried to storm the residence of a religious group known as the Branch Davidians. A gunfight broke out and there were deaths and injuries on both sides. On April 19, 1993, U.S. Attorney General Janet Reno, authorized the FBI to flush the Davidians out of their residence. A fire then broke out and seventy-six Davidians, including twenty-seven children, perished. Four BATF Agents; Todd McKeehan, Conway LeBleu, Robert Williams, and Steve Willis were killed.

Immigrations and Border Security
Immigrations and Border Security – Ineffective Border Security

In defense of the federal government, illegal immigration is difficult to measure. No one can provide exact figures on how many people are in the U.S. illegally. However, recent studies have shown a decline. The southern border, far from being "unsecured", is in better shape than it has been in years. Border security is now better managed and less porous. Border security has been the beneficiary of security-budget increases since September 11, 2001, which has helped slow the pace of illegal entries. Although violent crime has been rising in Mexico, it has decreased this side of the border. In counties along the Southwestern border, violent crime has dropped more than 30% in the past two decades. According to FBI statistics, the four safest big cities in the U.S. are San Diego, Phoenix, El Paso, and Austin; all of which are in Border States.

WHY ESTABLISH A NATIONAL POLICE AGENCY IF MOST AMERICANS WOULD NOT SUPPORT IT?

There are very few states without some form of consolidated or central government. Some transitions have worked well in eliminating wasteful spending practices, reduced operating costs, and reduced force strength without degrading capabilities (e.g., Metropolitan Las Vegas, Nevada, Nashville-Davidson County, Tennessee and Jacksonville-Duval County, Florida).

Establishing a National Police Agency would require massive start-up costs and may take years if not decades to realize fiscal efficiencies. However, operationally, the results would be almost immediate. Early assessments can determine if the agency will be successful in meeting core responsibilities.

Union Parish Sheriff Robert "Bob" Buckley (R)

Sheriff Robert Buckley

Two central questions were provided to the late Union Parish (LA) Sheriff Robert "Bob" Buckley on the issue of a National Police Agency which included the growth of law enforcement and if he supported a national agency, if not, why. Sheriff Buckley was well known, highly respected and regarded as a premier law enforcement officer in Louisiana and the southern region of the United States. He won four consecutive elections as

Sheriff of Union Parish. He does not support a national police and believes police services are localized and held accountable locally. He agreed with current structure and standing cooperative agreements with federal authorities. His response is noteworthy and provided in its entirety. He passed away in 2014 after a battle with cancer. (Appendix A)

Today, American law enforcement agencies are diversified in jurisdiction and responsibilities. Employers (hospitals, colleges, transit authorities, etc.) may have their own police. Most police departments (almost 90%) in the U.S. employ fewer than 50 sworn officers.

The rapid growth of the population, advent of the technical age and the super highway of information on the Internet make it more necessary for government intervention to protect the American government and her people while preserving the freedoms guaranteed by the Constitution.

※

CHAPTER 4 - CRIME IN THE U. S.

... less than 2% of the 40 million people who had contact with police reported the use of force or threatened use of force.

Use of Deadly Force

In recent years, state and local police agencies have been under intense scrutiny on the use of excessive or deadly force. Two recent reports from USA Today and ProPublica are provided below that discuss the ongoing issues primarily with local police agencies.

USE OF FORCE MODEL

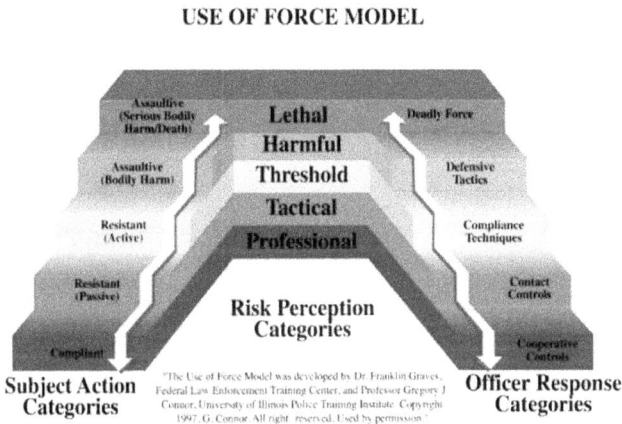

Assaultive (Serious Bodily Harm/Death)   **Lethal**   Deadly Force

Assaultive (Bodily Harm)   **Harmful**   Defensive Tactics

Threshold

Resistant (Active)   **Tactical**   Compliance Techniques

Professional

Resistant (Passive)   Contact Controls

Risk Perception Categories

Compliant   Cooperative Controls

Subject Action Categories   "The Use of Force Model was developed by Dr. Franklin Graves, Federal Law Enforcement Training Center, and Professor Gregory J Connor, University of Illinois Police Training Institute. Copyright 1997. G. Connor. All right reserved. Used by permission."   **Officer Response Categories**

In a recent study reported by USA Today (Heath, B., Johnson, K. & Hoyer, M., August 2014), according to the FBI, within a seven year period ending in 2012, a white police officer killed a black person nearly twice a week. (USA Today, August, 2014).

The reports show that 18% of the blacks killed during that seven year period were under the age of 21, compared to 8.7% of whites. These killings, whether justified or not, are self-reported by law enforcement and not all police departments participate so the database under counts the actual number of deaths. Furthermore, the numbers are not audited after they are submitted to the FBI. The statistics on "justifiable" homicides have conflicted with independent measures of fatalities at the hands of police.

In the report, almost 750 agencies contribute to the database which is a fraction of the over 17,000 law enforcement agencies that are in the U.S. Although not completely accurate, the FBI records remain the most complete nationwide accounting of people killed by the police.

The International Association of Chiefs of Police, the nation's largest group of police officials, has maintained that police use of force is rare. Citing data gathered by the Bureau of Justices Statistics in 2008, the IACP said less than 2% of the 40 million people who had contact with police reported the use of force or threatened use of force.

The report also stated that on average, there were 96 such incidents among at least 400 police killings each year that were reported to the FBI by local police. These numbers appear to show that Officer Darren Wilson shooting Michael Brown, a black teenager in Ferguson, Missouri, was not an isolated event in American policing.

In a report released by ProPublica (Gabrielson, R., Jones, R and Sagara, E., October 2014), in recent years young black males had a risk of being shot dead by police 21 times greater than their white counterparts. This statistic is according to federally collected data on fatal police shootings (ProPublica, 2014).

The report further states that the 1,217 deadly police shootings from 2010 to 2012 captured in the federal data show that blacks, age 15 to 19, were killed at a rate of 31.17 per million. Only 1.47 per million white males in that age range died at the hands of police.

The analysis shows that 185 more whites would have had to have been killed over those three years to have been at equal risk. The data is alarming; this equates to over one additional killing of a white male per week. (ProPublica, 2014).

ProPublica's risk analysis on young males killed by police suggests that blacks are being killed at disturbing rates when set against the rest of the American population. Their examination involved detailed accounts of more than 12,000 police homicides from 1980 to 2012 contained in the FBI's Supplementary Homicide Report. The data which is annually self-reported by hundreds of police departments across the country confirms some assumptions, but runs counter to other assumptions. It also adds nuance to a wide range of questions about the use of deadly police force.

According to ProPublica's report, the FBI's data has appeared in news accounts over the years. It surfaced again with the shooting of Michael Brown in Ferguson, Missouri in August 2014. To a great degree, observers and experts lamented the limited nature of the FBI's reports. Their shortcomings are inarguable.

Be aware that the data is incomplete. Enormous numbers of the country's 17,000+ police departments do not file fatal police shooting reports at all. Many have filed reports for some years, but not others. Florida departments have no filed reports since 1997 and New York City departments last reported in 2007. There is no systematic audit to verify the accuracy in the self-reporting.

However, there is value in what the data can show while accepting and accounting for its limitations. ProPublica's analysis included dividing the number of people of each race killed by police by the number of people of each race living in the country at the time. This produced two different rates which showed the risk of getting killed by police for whites and for blacks.

ProPublica spent weeks digging into the many categories of information in the reports hold. This included the race of the officers involved, the circumstances cited for the use of deadly force, and the age of those killed.

Who Gets Killed?

The data that young black men are 21 times as likely as their white peers to be killed by police is drawn from reports filed for the years 2010 to 2012. These are the three most recent years for which FBI numbers are available.

ProPublica stated that the black boys killed were sometimes disturbingly young. There were forty-one teens, ages 14 years or younger that were reported killed by police from 1980 to 2012. Twenty-seven of them were black; eight were white; four were Hispanic,; and one was Asian (ProPublica, 2014).

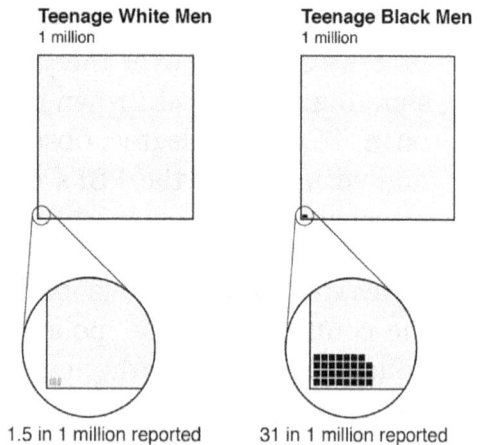

Teenage White Men
1 million

1.5 in 1 million reported

Teenage Black Men
1 million

31 in 1 million reported

Reported killings by police during 2010-2012
21 times as likely for black vs. white teenage men

This is not to imply that officers were not killing white people. According to ProPublica, at least 44 percent of all those killed by police across the 33 years were white. Whether white or black, those slain by police tended to be around the same age. The average age of blacks killed by police was 30. The average age of whites killed by police was 35.

Who is Killing All Those Black Men and Boys?

ProPublica's report suggests that mostly white officers are killing black men and boys. However, some instances reveal that black officers were also killing black men and boys. Black officers account for a little more than 10 percent of all fatal police shootings. Of those they killed, 78 percent were black.

White officers, given that they make up the majority of the country's police departments, are well represented in all categories of police killings. White officers killed 91 percent of whites. They were also responsible for 68 percent of the people of color killed. Those people of color represented 46 percent of all those killed by white officers.

What Were the Circumstances Surrounding All These Fatal Encounters?

There were 151 instances in which police noted that teens they had shot dead had been fleeing or resisting arrest at the time of the encounter. 67 percent of those killed in such circumstances were black. According to ProPublica, that disparity was even starker in previous years. Of the 15 teens that were shot fleeing arrest from 2010 to 2012, 14 were black.

Did police always list the circumstances of the killings? No, actually, there were many deadly shootings in which the circumstances were listed as "undetermined". 77 percent of those killed in such instances were black.

Certainly, there were instances where police truly feared for their lives. The data shows that police reported this as the cause of their actions in far greater numbers after the 1985

Supreme Court decision stating that police could only justify using deadly force if the suspects posed a threat to the officer or others. From 1980 to 1984, "officer under attack" was listed as the cause for 33 percent of the deadly shootings. Twenty years later, looking at data from 2005 to 2009, "officer under attack" was cited in 62 percent of police killings.

Does the Data Include Cases Where Police Killed People with Something Other Than a Standard Service Handgun?

Yes. The Los Angeles Police Department (LAPD) stood out in its use of shotguns. Most police killings involve officers firing handguns. From 1980 to 2012, 714 cases involved the use of a shotgun. The LAPD has a special claim on that category. It accounted for 47 cases in which an officer used a shotgun. The next highest total came from the Dallas Police Department (DPD) with 14 cases.

ProPublica calculated a statistical figure, called a risk ratio, by dividing the rate of black homicide victims by the rate of white homicide victims. This ratio, commonly used in epidemiology, gives an estimate of how much more at risk black teenagers were of being killed by police officers. Risk ratios may have vary in levels of precision, depending on a variety of mathematical factors.

In this case, because such shootings are rare from a statistical perspective, a 95 percent confidence interval indicates that black teenagers are at between 10 and 40 times greater risk of being killed by a police officer. The calculation used the 2010-2012 population estimates from the U.S. Census Bureau's American Community Survey.

Crime in the United States

Enforcement of criminal laws in the U.S. is determined by jurisdiction. This includes local ordinances, state criminal codes, and tribal and federal offenses. An example of a typical annual crime analysis is provided below for the calendar year 2009. Detailed and annual crime analysis can be found on the Federal Bureau of Investigations' (FBI) web-site http://www.fbi.gov/ucr/ucr.htm under the Uniform Crime Reporting (UCR) Program and United States Department of Justice (DOJ) Bureau of Statistics website http://bjs.ojp.usdoj.gov/.

The UCR Program defines violent crimes as murder, non-negligent manslaughter, forcible rape, robbery, and aggravated assault. These crimes are committed using force or threat of force. The information below summarizes the national statistics on violent crime according to the UCR Program (UCR, 2010).

Overview of National Statistics – Violent Crime

- In 2009, an estimated 1,318,398 violent crimes occurred nationwide, a decrease of

- 5.3% from the 2008 estimate.

- When considering 5 and 10 year trends, the 2009 estimated violent crime total was 5.2% below the 2005 level and 7.5% below the 2000 level.

- There were an estimated 429.4 violent crimes per 100,000 inhabitants in 2009.

- Aggravated assaults accounted for the highest number of violent crimes reported to law enforcement at 61.2%. Robbery comprised 31% of violent crimes, forcible rape accounted for 6.7%, and murder accounted for 1.2% of estimated violent crimes in 2009.

- Information collected regarding type of weapon showed that firearms were used in

- 67.1% of the nation's murders, 42.6% of robberies, and 20.9% of aggravated assaults. (Weapons' data are not collected for forcible rape)

Overview of National Statistics - Murder

- An estimated 15,241 persons were murdered nationwide in 2009, which is a 7.3% decrease from the 2008 estimate, a 9.0% decrease from the 2005 estimate, and a

- 2.2% decrease from the 2000 estimate.

- There were 5 murders per 100,000 inhabitants in 2009, an 8.1% decrease from the 2008 rate. Compared with the 2005 rate there was a 12.1% decrease in the murder rate. Compared with the 2000 rate there was a 10.4% decrease was recorded.

- More than 44% of murders were reported in the South, the most populous region, with 21.3% reported in the West, 20.0% reported in the Midwest, and 13.9% reported in the Northeast.

Overview of National Statistics – Forcible Rape

- In 2009, the number of forcible rapes was estimated at 88,097. By comparison, the estimated volume of rapes for 2009 was 2.6%

lower than the 2008 estimate, 6.6% lower than the 2005 number, and 2.3% below the 2000 level.

- The rate of forcible rapes in 2009 was estimated at 56.6 per 100,000 female inhabitants, a 3.4% decrease when compared with the 2008 estimated rate of 58.6.

- Rapes by force comprised 93% of reported rape offenses in 2009 and attempts or assaults to commit rape accounted for 7% of reported rapes.

Overview of National Statistics - Robbery

- In 2009, there were an estimated 408,217 robberies nationwide.

- The estimated number of robberies decreased from the 2008 and the 2005 estimates from 8% to 2.2%, respectively. However, the 2009 robbery estimate increased slightly from the 2000 estimate.

- The 2009 estimated robbery rate of 133 per 100,000 inhabitants reflected a decrease of 8.8% when compared with the 2008 rate.

- An estimated $508 million in losses were attributed to robberies in 2009.

- The average dollar value of property stolen per reported robbery was $1,244. The highest average dollar loss was for banks; which lost $4,029 per offense.

Firearms were used in 42.6% of the robberies for which the UCR Program received additional information in 2009. Strong-arm tactics were used in 41.1% of the total number of robberies, knives and cutting instruments were used in 7.7%, and other dangerous weapons were used in 8.7% of robberies in 2009.

Overview of National Statistics – Aggravated Assault

- There were an estimated 806,843 aggravated assaults in the nation in 2009.

- According to 2 and 10 year trend data, the estimated number of aggravated assaults in 2009 declined 4.2% from 2008 and 11.5% when compared with the estimate for 2000.

- In 2009, the estimated rate of aggravated assaults was 262.8 offenses per 100,000 inhabitants.

- A 10 year comparison of data from 2000 and 2009 showed that the rate of aggravated assaults in 2009 dropped 18.9%.

- Of the aggravated assault offenses in 2009 for which law enforcement agencies provided expanded data; 26.9% were committed with hands, fists, and feet; 20.9% were committed with firearms; and 18.7% were committed with knives or cutting instruments. The remaining 33.5% of aggravated assaults were committed with other weapons.

Correctional Population in the U.S.
2008 Correctional Population:

- Over 7.3 million people on probation, in jail or prison, or on parole at year end consisted of 3.2% of all U.S. adult residents or 1 in every 31 adults.

- Over 70% of the persons under correctional supervision were supervised in the community either on probation or parole, while 30% were incarcerated in the nation's prisons or jails.

- Over 4,270,917 adult men and women on probation and 828,169 on parole or mandatory conditional release following a prison term.

- State and federal prison authorities had jurisdiction over 1,610,446 prisoners: 1,409,166 in state jurisdiction and 201,280 in federal jurisdiction.

- Local jails held 785,556 persons awaiting trial, or serving a sentence. An additional 72,852 persons under jail supervision were serving their sentence in the community.

- The U.S. has the highest documented incarceration rate in the world at 754 persons in prison or jail per 100,000 U.S. residents (as of 2008). More than 1 in 100 adults in the U.S. are in prison. The U.S. has less than 5% of the world's population and 23.4% of the world's prison population.

By comparison in 2006, the incarceration rate in England and Wales was 148 persons imprisoned per 100,000 residents. The rate for Norway was 66 inmates per 100,000 and the rate for New Zealand was 186 per 100,000. In Australia in 2005, the rate was 126 prisoners per 100,000 residents. In the Netherlands, the 2002 rate was 93 per 100,000.

Correctional Comparison

United States and International Prisons

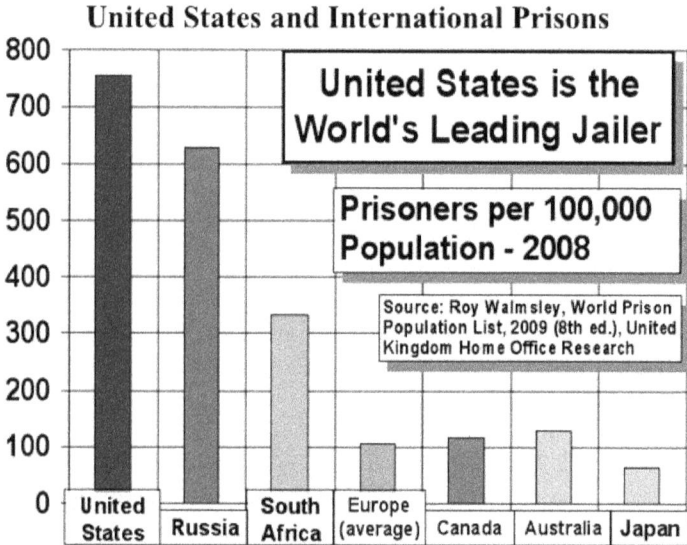

United States is the World's Leading Jailer

Prisoners per 100,000 Population - 2008

Source: Roy Walmsley, World Prison Population List, 2009 (8th ed.), United Kingdom Home Office Research

| United States | Russia | South Africa | Europe (average) | Canada | Australia | Japan |

Comparisons of Prisons in US and other International

Capital Punishment
(United States of America)

Thirty five states and the federal government had capital statutes by the end of 2013. More than 3,200 inmates are on death row in the U.S. awaiting execution.

The state of Virginia executed Teresa Lewis at 9:13 pm on September 23, 2010 for arranging the execution of her husband and stepson for a $250,000 insurance policy. Lewis was the first female executed in the U.S. in five years and in the state of Virginia in 100 years. In 2014, seven states executed 35 inmates which was 4 less than in 2013. As of December 31, 2013, all 35 states with death penalty statutes authorized lethal injection as a method of execution (BJS, 2014).

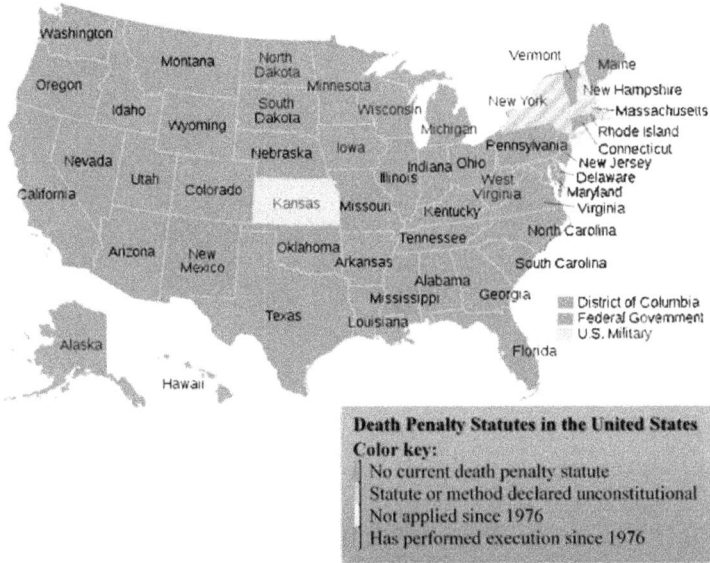

Death Penalty Statutes in the United States
Color key:
No current death penalty statute
Statute or method declared unconstitutional
Not applied since 1976
Has performed execution since 1976

Capital Punishment (Death Row) since 1976

Jurisdiction	Executions	On Death Row
USA Federal Government (including the Armed Forces)	3	63
Texas, Louisiana, Mississippi, Alabama, Georgia, Arkansas, Florida, North & South Carolina, Missouri, Tennessee and Virginia	966	1815
Oklahoma, Ohio, Indiana, Kentucky, Nebraska, Colorado, Montana, Idaho, Kansas, South Dakota	181	317
Arizona, California, Nevada, Utah, Washington, Oregon, New Mexico, Wyoming	55	1003
Delaware, Maryland, Pennsylvania, Connecticut, New Hampshire	23	204
Total	1,238	3,402

Past Executions and Inmates on Death Row in the U.S.

Supreme Court rulings on a lawyer's duty

What the Supreme Court said in important cases dealing with ineffective assistance of counsel in death row sentencing cases:

NO DEFENSE: Shortcut to Death Row

1984
Case can be overturned if lawyer's performance is poor

Strickland v. Washington Defendants can get convictions or sentences overturned if they prove their lawyers' performance was substandard, that a better performance would have resulted in a different verdict

Justices don't define ineffectiveness beyond "reasonableness under prevailing professional norms"

2000
Client's awful past must be investigated

Williams v. Taylor Court finds, for the first time, that failure to investigate a client's awful background amounts to ineffective assistance of counsel; entitles inmate to new sentencing

Attorney's failure to research Williams' nightmarish childhood was unreasonable

2003
A cursory background investigation ineffective

Wiggins v. Smith Defendant denied his right to counsel by attorneys who failed to research his background

Attorneys have obligation to "discover all reasonably mitigating evidence" that could be used to defend clients

2005
Lawyers must follow up on all evidence regarding awful past

Rompilla v. Beard Court says, for third time, a death row inmate's lawyers failed him in courtroom by not following up on leads discovered about his awful past

© 2007 MCT
Source: McClatchy Washington Bureau
Graphic: Lee Hulteng, Judy Treible

※

CHAPTER 5 - CONSOLIDATION EFFORTS: CASE STUDIES

Consolidation Efforts: Lessons Learned

Consolidation models look good on paper. However, developing and successfully implementing a new program may prove to be more difficult. How would success be defined?

Success would be defined in part by realization of cost efficiencies over the long-term, dramatic reductions in personnel and infrastructure, immediate improvement in policing, investigative services and public safety, development of national standards, nonpartisan oversight standards, and, most importantly, acceptance by the American people.

Police departments' costs would steadily increase as the population continues to rise. More people require more policing and services. As of 2011, consolidating police departments has become a practical means to deal with routinely increased financial burdens placed on individual agencies.

Consolidation studies conducted over many years show advantages and disadvantages of merging police departments into metropolitan (Las Vegas, Nevada) or regional forces (Berks-Lehigh Regional Police Department – Pennsylvania). However, there are few studies available on nationalizing police services. Such an agency would be among the largest federal police agencies in the world with more than 350,000 sworn officers. This would be about one third of the total number of sworn law enforcement officers today. The following is a brief snapshot of the U.S. profile including territories under U.S. control:

US Population: 310,209,236

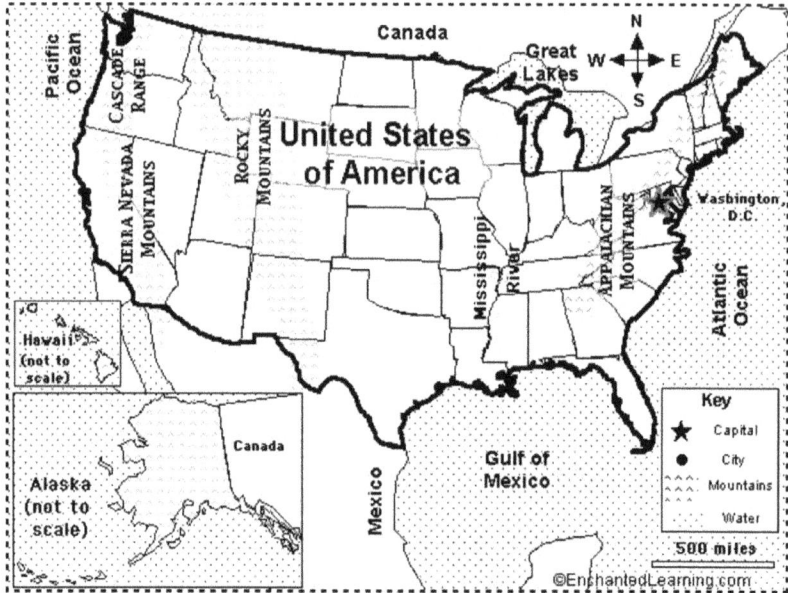

United States of America and Historic Landmarks

The 48 contiguous states that make up the continental United States (CONUS) are located in North America between Mexico and Canada. The state of Hawaii is located in the Pacific Ocean, midway between North America and Asia. The state of Alaska is located on the extreme northwest corner of North America. The U.S. also controls a number of small islands in the Caribbean and the Pacific. The U.S. is the third largest country in the world in area behind Russia and Canada. It has a total area of 3,717,792 square miles. This total includes the 50 states and the District of Columbia (Washington, DC), but not U.S. territories and dependencies. Of this territory, there are 3,536,274 square miles of land, while there are 181,517 square miles of water.

The U.S. is about one-half the size of Russia and slightly larger than either Brazil or China. It shares long borders with both Canada (5,526 miles) and Mexico (2,066 miles). The nation's total borders are 7,610 miles long. Eastern U.S. borders the Atlantic Ocean and Caribbean Sea, while the West Coast borders the Pacific Ocean. Areas of Alaska border the Arctic Ocean. In all, U.S. has 12,380 miles of coastline.

U.S.'s capital is Washington, D.C., (DC) located on the East Coast, almost midway between Maine and Florida. DC has a population of 519,000. America's largest cities are New York, with a population of 7,428,162, followed by Los Angeles with 3,633,591, and Chicago with 2,799,050.

Two Points of View to Justify a Debate on Creating a System that Works Efficiently, Less Politics, Mission Focused, and Fiscally Sound Are Provided Below.

Case Study One - Regionalization/Consolidation within State/Local Jurisdictions

San Diego Police Department

San Diego is internationally known as America's Finest City because of its unique climate, beaches, and world class tourist attractions. San Diego is home to the National Football League (NFL) San Diego Chargers and Major League Baseball (MLB) San Diego Padres. San Diego offers a vibrant and diverse economy along with a strong and committed public/private partnership of local government and businesses dedicated to the creation and retention of quality jobs for its residents.

The city is also situated in a unique and vulnerable region because of its close proximity to the Mexican border. It is also home to one of the largest military complexes in the world. No other location in the U.S. is a better model for regionalization or consolidation than San Diego County.

San Diego County, one of 58 counties in the state of California, was established on February 18, 1850, just after California became the 31st state. The county stretches 65 miles from north to south and 86 miles from east to west, covering 4,261 square miles. Elevation ranges from sea level to about 6,500 feet. Orange and Riverside counties border it to the north, the agricultural communities of Imperial County to the east, the Pacific Ocean to the west and the state of Baja California and Mexico to the south.

San Diego County is comprised of 18 incorporated cities and 17 unincorporated communities. The county's total population in 2009 was approximately 3.17 million with a median age of 35 years (California Department of Finance Report E-1: City/County Population Estimates). San Diego is the third most populous county in the state.

Unlike most major cities in recent time, San Diego had a declining crime rate from 1990 to 2000. Crime slightly increased in the early 2000s. In 2004, San Diego had the sixth lowest crime rate of any U.S. city with over a million residents. From 2002 to 2006, the crime rate overall dropped 0.8%, though not evenly by category. While violent crime decreased 12.4% during this period, property crime increased 1.1%. Total property crimes were lower than the national average in 2004.

Military bases in San Diego include U.S. Navy (USN) ports, U.S. Marine Corps (USMC) bases, and U.S. Coast Guard (USCG) stations. Marine Corps bases in San Diego include Marine Corps Air Station (MCAS) Miramar, Marine Corps

Base (MCB), Camp Pendleton, and Marine Corps Recruit Depot (MCRD) San Diego.

The Navy has several major commands and installations in San Diego including, Commander, Naval Air Forces Pacific (COMNAVAIRPAC), Commander, Naval Surface Forces Pacific (COMNAVSURFPAC), Commander Third Fleet (COMTHIRDFLEET), Commander, Navy Installations Command (CNIC) and shore installations: Naval Base Point Loma (formerly Recruit/Navy Training Command and Submarine Base San Diego), Naval Base San Diego (also known as 32nd Street Naval Station), Naval Base Coronado (formerly known as Naval Air Station North Island and Naval Amphibious Base Coronado), Bob Wilson Naval Hospital, and the Space and Naval Warfare Systems Center San Diego.

San Diego is home to one of the largest naval fleets in the world and has become the largest concentration of naval facilities in the world due to base reductions in Norfolk, Virginia and retrenchment of the Russian naval base in Vladivostok. Two of the U.S. Navy's Nimitz Class Nuclear Powered Super Aircraft Carriers, (USS Carl Vinson CVN-70 and USS Ronald Reagan CVN-76), five amphibious assault ships, several Los Angeles Class "fast attack" submarines, the Hospital Ship USNS MERCY, carrier and submarine tenders, destroyers, cruisers, frigates, and many smaller ships. Four Navy vessels have been named USS SAN DIEGO in honor of the city.

There are at least 19 separate law enforcement agencies in San Diego County. Each operate in autonomy from the other including their own local government supporting and funding.

Law Enforcement Agencies in San Diego County

Carlsbad Police Department
Employees – 162
Budget - $27,300,000

La Mesa Police Department
Employees - 21
Budget - $2,581,130

Chula Vista Police Department
Employees - 360
Budget - $44,957,802

National City Police Department
Employees - 139
Budget - $16,666,130

Coronado Police Department
Employees - 67
Budget - $14,175,000

Oceanside Police Department
Employees - 321
Budget $36,440,800

El Cajon Police Department
Employees - 203
Budget - $28,985,707

San Diego Harbor Police Department
Employees - 173
Budget $29,253,800

Escondido Police Department
Employees - 265
Budget $34,640,665

San Diego Police Department
Employees – 2,755
Budget - $409,325,900

School, College, and University Police Departments
+700 employees with total budgets exceeding $50M

- University of California San Diego Police
- San Diego City Schools Police
- San Diego Community College Police
- San Diego State University Police
- California State University San Marcos Police
- Grossmont Community College Police
- Palomar Community College Police
- Southwestern Community College Police

San Diego County Sheriff's Department

- 4000 employees: 2000 volunteers: $566 million annual budget

- Provides contract law enforcement services to the cities of Del Mar, Encinitas, Solana Beach, Imperial Beach, Lemon Grove, Poway, Santee, San Marcos and Vista

- Coordinate with 17 Native American jurisdictions

- Total (funds used to support law enforcement): $1.26B

- Total (personnel supporting law enforcement): 9166 employees

- Population within Jurisdiction: 4,261 square miles and 3.17M people

San Diego County Law Enforcement Compared to Other Major Agencies in California

Comparative Analysis of Law Enforcement in California Major Jurisdictions

Agency	Employees	Area of Coverage square mile	Annual Budget	Population	Assigned
LA Police Department	12,982	470	$1.4 Billion	4,004,000	Police Commission (Board) – Chief reports to Board
LA County Sheriff Department	19,000 (largest Sheriff's Dept. worldwide)	4,084	$2,540,388,000	10,347,437	Sheriff (elected position county wide)
SF Police Department	2,361	231.93	$365 Million	880,000	Police Commission – Chief of Police (appointed) reports to Police Commission
SF County Sheriff Department	950	232	N/A	880,000	Sheriff (primary role is managing jails and limited services)

Continue On Next Page

(CONTINUED) San Diego County Law Enforcement Comparative

Agency	Employees	Area of Coverage square mile	Annual Budget	Population	Assigned
Oakland Police Department	1140	53.8	$183,315,150	420,183	Chief of Police (appointed)
Alameda County Sheriff Department	1500	737.57	$135 Million	1,526,148	Sheriff (elected position county wide)
Riverside County Sheriff Department	3000	7303	$542,334,149	2,100,516	Sheriff (elected position county wide)

The U.S. Navy met similar choices at the end of the Cold War with the emergence of new threats including Asymmetric Warfare. In Navy terms, this would be a "brown water" threat. For decades, the Navy focused on "blue water" threats, meaning on the high seas and over the horizon. The Navy needed a realistic and cost prohibitive way to downsize and modernize the Fleet without degrading war fighting capabilities.

In October 2003, the Chief of Naval Operations (CNO) established Navy Installations Command (CNIC) with complete responsibility for Navy-wide shore installation management. The stand-up of CNIC reduced the Navy's major claimants from 18 to 1. A major sea change in the way shore installations would be managed to deal with the changing post 9/11 environment.

The intent of CNIC is to establish a single shore installation management organization that will focus on installation effectiveness and improve the shore installation management community's ability to support the fleet and eliminate wasteful spending on unnecessary systems and force structure. Some of the successes included the following (CNIC, 2010):

- Regionally centered processes (de-layered)
    - Aligned all installations under 11 Regions (San Diego – Southwest Region)
    - Functions centered regionally or at Headquarters e.g., Housing, Morale, Welfare, and Recreation
    - Combined bases/staffs, e.g.,, Naval Air Station North Island, Norfolk, Virginia, Port Hueneme, California, Bremerton, Washington, and Guam
- Consolidated "back of house"/common support functions for Continental United States (CONUS) community support programs, improving expertise and saving up to 15% across the board
    - Streamlined Comptroller organization
    - One (1) Comptroller vs. 20
- Standardized processes and work flow, new single financial system
- Consolidated cell phone contracts from 233 to 3 (-47%)
- Reduced Information Technology (IT) applications from 1842 to 335 (-82%)
- 51% reduction in number of IT servers
- Prototype for wireless pier connectivity
- Reduced legacy networks 44% (121 to 67)
- Reduced dual desktops by 66% (957 to 319)

How Did the Navy Achieve Success and is the Plan Working Today?

The Navy used a "Program Centric Resourcing and Execution" approach. This approach includes managing the enterprise and executing the mission under a Program Centric Model versus an Installation Centric Model of the past. This process involves a different perspective and philosophy. It centralizes program management and direction at the CNIC Headquarters Program Director (HPD) level with execution through Regional Program Directors.

This approach also includes elimination of layering and duplication of effort between installations, regions, and at headquarters. Thus, reducing resource requirements while increasing efficiencies. Simply put, this is about putting the meat on the bones of the future concept. It includes documenting processes, streamlining processes, eliminating non-value added variability in the work/steps/ processes and maximizing distance support.

Navy leadership sent a clear message to the fleet to get rid of unnecessary practices and programs. The fleet was to develop means to perform necessary work in the most efficient manner and determine where and by whom the necessary work can most effectively and efficiently be performed. Navy officials evaluated numerous processes and management tools before finding the right fit for the right force structure.

Today, the regionalization concept continues to achieve success and is being studied by other agencies as a model. CNIC encompasses 11 Regional Commands worldwide and 77 naval shore installations within the following regions:

- Commander, Naval District Washington, Washington, DC

- Commander, Navy Region Mid-Atlantic, Norfolk, VA

- Commander, Navy Region Midwest, Great Lakes, IL

- Commander, Navy Region Northwest, Bremerton, WA

- Commander, Navy Region Southeast, Jacksonville, FL

- Commander, Navy Region Southwest, San Diego, CA

- Commander, Navy Region Europe-Africa-Southwest Asia, Naples, Italy

- Commander, Navy Region Hawaii, Honolulu, HI

- Commander, Navy Region Japan, Yokosuka, Japan

- Commander, Navy Region Korea, Seoul, South Korea

- Commander, Navy Region Marianas, Guam

- Area Coordinator, Singapore (not a region)

Although this is only a small example of successes achieved by regionalization, San Diego area governments should consider similar bold steps in the near future.

What are Some Strategies San Diego May Consider Using to Better Organize Emergency Services?

San Diego local governments should consider similar programs used by the Navy and other densely populated jurisdictions across the nation. San Francisco is an example; being the only consolidated City-County government in the state of California.

Specifically, City-County governments could consolidate all fire departments and districts within San Diego County under a single Fire Chief or a Board of Directors (North Region/County, West Region/County, East Region/County, South Region/County and a Chairman). All police agencies could consolidate under one Sheriff or Police Commission;

either option should be an elected office county wide. Such a consolidation could have the following benefits:

- Eliminate duplicative services (multiple Fire, Police, Homeland Security Departments)
- Reduce high administration to operation cost ratios
- Replace outdated or deteriorating infrastructure and equipment
- Reduce inventories of underutilized equipment, buildings or facilities
- Redraw overlapping or inefficient service boundaries
- Replace inefficient purchasing or budgeting practices
- Implement economies of scale
- Increase profitable outsourcing

Unlike many jurisdictions in California, San Diego has the capacity, resources, infrastructure, and political will to protect and serve the community. Like any system, events can overwhelm a local government's ability to protect the people. When this happens, as in the case of the 2007 wildfires, the state and federal governments have a duty to respond with swift dispatch and all resources available to contain the event. The local elected government official is usually the person in charge, unless another official has been designated through ordinance or legislation. This can be complicated in San Diego with so many incorporated cities and unincorporated communities in San Diego County.

Elected and appointed officials at the local level include mayors, county executives, city and county council members, and commissioners. They shoulder the obligation of political responsiveness in disaster and emergency events. Appointed officials, like city managers, have important political and managerial duties in the disaster management realm. These officials are responsible for hazards and emergency management policy formulation and oversight.

A crucial element involved in creating any regional fire protection system or police agency, is determining how it will be governed. For example, will the new system be governed by an appointed or elected board? If elected, should board members be selected at large or by division? How many members should make up the board? Should there be advisory committees? What name should be given to the new entity?

Option 1 (Law Enforcement): Merge all law enforcement agencies in San Diego County, including college campus police and consolidate under the San Diego County Police. Establish a police commission, no more than five members and each position elected county wide. San Diego Sheriff becomes Chief Executive for the County Police and reports to the Police Commission.

Listed below are several advantages in consolidation and regionalization for the San Diego area governments:

- Greater efficiency by providing the most effective means for streamlining the delivery of service

- Simplifies budgeting, fiscal operations

- Greater flexibility in the use of Department resources and assets

- More effective use of executive management

- A single police agency best accommodates special tax election initiatives for police protection service

Organizational Approach

Merge all incorporated and unincorporated government entities into one government, City of San Diego. This would include San Diego absolving the 17 cities and 17 unincorporated governments and the county government. Government would be a strong Mayor government with a county wide City Council (County Supervisors would become Council Members and continue to be elected as representatives of their districts). Council membership would be decided based on districts and regions within the county. The entire county of San Diego would become the City of San Diego.

Merge all Law Enforcement agencies (including college campus police) within San Diego County under one agency, San Diego Metropolitan Police. Establish a Police Commission (elected) and transfer Sheriff (elected) to Chief Executive Officer reporting to the Police Commission. Essentially, San Diego County Sheriff would absolve all police agencies within the county and rename department to reflect merger of governments, San Diego Metropolitan Police.

San Diego area governments cannot continue to bankroll bloated bureaucracies and high pension and health insurance costs. This new economic reality forces a conversation that can no longer be ignored and continue to deliver services as in the past. Consolidation and regionalization rather than duplication, is not only cheaper, but more efficient in terms of coordination.

Emergency services and crime must be dealt with regionally because they know no boundaries. Consolidation, standardization and regionalization means reducing bureaucracy, streamlining government and creating better enforcement and better coordination of resources.

Case Study Two – Failure of Critical Institutions

New Orleans Police Department

The New Orleans Police Department (NOPD) has a sustained history of corruption with repeated demonstrations of inability to self-govern. What happens when a critical institution fails? Is it the state's responsibility or the federal government to restore order? This study enters the formally corrupt world of the NOPD. Out of control, NOPD was filled with crooked cops, some of whom even had been jailed for their crimes. In 1994, New Orleans elected a new Mayor, Marc Morial. The top of his agenda was a promise to clean up the police department.

Morial understood the enormity of the task and admitted that cleaning up NOPD would be his greatest challenge. Over the next eight years of his administration, he made true to his promise in cleaning up NOPD. However, within months of his departure, NOPD returned to its roots of corruption. During Hurricane Katrina, this institution collapsed and lost control of the city.

NOPD'S LONG HISTORY OF SCANDAL

November 1980 Violence in Algiers

NOPD Officer Neupert is found shot to death near his patrol car in Algiers. Blaming his death on local drug dealers, officers respond with what historian Leonard Moore calls "domestic terrorism," killing four civilians (James Billy, Jr., Reginald Miles, Sherry Lynn Singleton, and Raymond Ferdinand) and injuring 50 in their hunt for the killer. An Algiers' housing project resident, who witnessed the police roundup, told the Associated Press: "They didn't give any warning ... just started grabbing boys. <u>Civil Rights Lawyer, Mary Howell,</u> represented Algiers citizens who filed civil lawsuits against NOPD. Mary Howell discovered that basic police procedures including report writing -- had been abandoned during the days after Neupert's death. "We had trouble identifying where all officers were ... but it also meant officers couldn't account for what they were doing."

In 1983, following a federal probe, seven officers, known as the "Algiers 7", were indicted. Three were convicted of violating the civil rights of four civilians during interrogations. Charges were never filed relating to the four civilian deaths.

In April 1986, the City of New Orleans paid roughly $2.8 million to settle lawsuits filed by citizens alleging mistreatment.

March 22, 1990 Officer Killed; Police Vow Revenge

Adolph Archie, a petty criminal, escapes from a work release program. While trying to steal a car, he assaults a security guard, takes her gun, and runs. **NOPD Officer Earl Hauck** chases him. In a standoff, Archie shoots Hauck four times, killing him. Pursued by other officers, Archie is shot in the arm and apprehended. While he's being driven to the hospital, mobs of officers line the streets threatening to kill Archie. Radio scanners record officers encouraging violence.

Instead of going to the hospital, the police bring Archie to the First District police station – Officer Hauck's home station. It is unclear what happens there. Some officers have reported a scuffle. Archie eventually is transported to the hospital, where x-rays are taken (and subsequently lost). He is injected with iodine to which he's allergic. Archie dies 13 hours later.

Coroner Paul Minyard, initially, rules his death to be consistent with a bad fall. Another autopsy, initiated by Mary Howell, representing Archie's family, indicates Archie was beaten to death. Minyard then changes the cause of death to "homicide by police intervention."

Orleans Parish investigates the incident for six months before clearing the officers involved. The NOPD pays Archie's family $333,000 in damages. This is one-third of which is designated for Officer Hauck's family following a wrongful death lawsuit.

Frank Minyard, MD
Orleans Parish Coroner

Civil rights attorney Howell describes Archie's death as "the beginning of the end for this police department, the fact that this could happen in broad daylight, openly". Warren Riley, former NOPD Chief of Police, who was then a young officer, remembers the incident differently. He stated that Adolph Archie did in fact steal an officer's weapon and he did kill a police officer. "There's some skepticism on whether Adolph Archie died in the hospital as it relates to something medically, something a doctor did, or something a police officer did. There are two sides to that story", he continued.

Early 1990's Peak of NOPD's Brutality and Corruption

NOPD's problems draw national attention. *The New York Times Magazine* published an article in March 1996 describing the NOPD as "The Thinnest Blue Line." It noted New Orleans as the nation's homicide capital in 1992 and 1994. According to the article, the NOPD solved just 37% of murders which is roughly half the national average. It is also reported that federal officials estimate that 10 to 15% of the force is corrupt.

The Times points to one root of the corruption being the culture of moonlighting and private security details, often at bars or strip clubs. This is due to the NOPD's low salaries. In 1993, new officers made less than $20,000 per year.

According to historian, Leonard Moore, the culture becomes one of "pseudo-organized crime". Moore also adds, "the allegiance becomes to this seedy, after-hours establishment that you are guarding ... as opposed to your particular shift at the precinct".

In 1993, the NOPD's vice squad is essentially disbanded after allegations of theft and shakedowns in New Orleans nightclubs and massage parlors. Nine of its twelve members are assigned to desk jobs within other police units. That same year, two officers are charged with raping a woman they arrested. By the end of the year, seventeen officers had been arrested or convicted of various crimes.

October 1994 – New Leadership in the City and the Police Department

Departing from New Orleans tradition, new Mayor Marc Morial brings in Richard Pennington, Assistant Chief of Washington DC Metropolitan Police Department, to lead the NOPD. Pennington's new policies shake up the force. Officers were no longer allowed to work details at bars and strip clubs. In addition, rules governing gift-giving to superiors were tightened and applicants with criminal records or bad credit would no longer be hired. At least 100 police officers were fired during Chief Pennington's eight-year stint.

October 13, 1994 Officer Len Davis Caught On Tape Ordering a Hit on a Civilian

New Orleans resident, Kim Marie Groves, witnesses Officer Davis beating up a neighborhood teenager. She files a formal complaint with the police. Within hours, a colleague tells Davis about Groves' allegations. The next night Groves is shot dead in front of her house. Davis had planned the hit. It was inadvertently recorded by federal officials who were investigating a cocaine ring involving Davis.

Len Davis
NOPD Officer
(Victim) Kim Groves

Davis had a reputation for being both roguish, but a good cop. Between 1987 and 1992, he received twenty complaints and was suspended six times. He was also awarded the NOPD's second highest honor in 1993, the Medal of Merit. Tried and sentenced to death for Groves' murder, Davis remains on death row. He is one of nine officers later indicted on federal weapons and drug charges for their participation in the cocaine ring. A half dozen officers, including Davis, were convicted.

Mayor Morial and Chief Pennington asked the FBI to work with the NOPD on its corruption problems. It is the only such arrangement in the country. The agreement also included the Department of Justice, the U.S. Marines, and the Louisiana State Police. One major focus of the agreement is to educate department heads on leadership and management. In addition, all NOPD officers receive training on values, ethics, and sensitivity.

March 4, 1995 Officer Kills Civilians and Former Partner

On this night, Officer Antoinette Frank was eating at a Vietnamese restaurant where she had once done private security detail work. Hours later, she returns with civilian Rogers LaCaze to rob the establishment. Frank and LaCaze shoot and kill Frank's former partner, Officer Ronald Williams, who was working security at the restaurant. They also kill several members of the Vu family, the restaurant's owners.

Antoinette Franks
NOPD Officer

Chau Vu, who was a teenager, survived by hiding in a cooler during the robbery. When the call went out that there had been a shooting, Frank returns to the restaurant to supposedly help in the investigation. Chau Vu identifies Frank as the shooter. Frank was then arrested, tried, and convicted of first-degree murder. Sentenced to death in September 1995, she remains on death row. LaCaze was also convicted of murder and sentenced to death row.

Disturbing details later emerged about Frank. She had failed two psychological exams before being admitted to the police academy. A supervisor had recommended that she return to the academy for more training. It was found that she also had stolen the gun used in the murders from the NOPD evidence room.

Spring 2002 - A New Mayor and a New Chief of Police

Chief Pennington ran for mayor of New Orleans, but lost to Ray Nagin, Cox Communications executive, who received the support of the police union.

Nagin named NOPD veteran, Eddie Compass, as chief of police. NOPD critics condemned this appointment, asserting that tapping an insider will virtually erase the progress that was made during Pennington's eight years of leadership.

August 1, 2005 NOPD Officers Suspected In Beating Death

A month before Hurricane Katrina hits, Raymond Robair, a Treme resident with a record of drug dealing and possession, is brought to a hospital by New Orleans police. He was suffering from severe injuries, including several broken ribs and a ruptured spleen. The officers told hospital staff they saw him "stumbling and holding his upper chest area" before collapsing on the street. Robair dies at the hospital. Coroner Frank Minyard rules the death was accidental based primarily on the police report, which is filed as a response to a medical incident.

Treme residents who witnessed the event, however, gave a very different account. They said that Robair was beaten by police. According to a July 2010 Times-Picayune article, numerous people reported that they witnessed police punch, kick, and stomp Robair. They stated that police chased Robair, beat him, and then ushered him away in the back of a police car. After Hurricane Katrina strikes New Orleans, Robair's case is momentarily forgotten.

Two years later, Mary Howell, the Robair family's attorney, has an independent autopsy performed by Dr. Kris Sperry, Georgia's chief medical examiner. He rules that Robair's death was a homicide. The case was brought before the district attorney in 2007 and subsequently dismissed. The FBI continued investigating the incident.

In July 2010, Officers Melvin Williams and Matthew Dean Moore were both indicted on federal charges related to Robair's death. Williams plead innocent to charges of beating Robair and obstructing justice under the federal deprivation of civil rights statute. Moore plead innocent to obstruction and lying to the FBI.

August 29, 2005 Hurricane Katrina Strikes; NOPD is Overwhelmed

Law enforcement confronted enormous logistical challenges such as power outages, flooded police headquarters, and a broken police radio system. Emergency 911 dispatchers received more than 600 calls within 20 minutes of the first levee breach. Focused on search and rescue operations, police set up temporary headquarters at Harrah's Casino. Boats were launched to rescue both civilians and officers, many of whom had been trapped in their homes or temporary command posts.

August 30, 2010 Civilian Shoots Officer; Widespread Looting; NOPD Feels under Siege

After stopping to pat down four men outside a looted Algiers gas station, Officer Kevin Thomas is shot in the head by one of the men, Jamil Joyner. It was the most high-profile act of violence against a police officer during the days following Hurricane Katrina and contributes to rumors of rampant civilian aggression toward law enforcement. Joyner is convicted of attempted first-degree murder in January 2010. Officer Thomas had to have four plates and sixteen screws in his head and continues to suffer from seizures and vision problems.

When told about Officer Thomas' shooting, Mayor Nagin was furious. According to Press Secretary, Sally Forman, "he (Nagin) said we need to declare martial law." He continued to say, "we are dealing with search and rescue, we're dealing with saving lives...if some thugs are going to go after our cops, then we're going after them".

Traumatized by the storm, two NOPD officers, Lawrence Celestine and Paul Accardo committed suicide within days of one another in early September. On September 5, The Boston Globe quoted Chief Compass as saying "the world can't understand what has happened in New Orleans in recent days".

September 1, 2005 Motionless Bodies Photographed on Religious Street

Times-Picayune reporter Gordon Russell and freelance photographer Marko Georgiev encountered and photographed officers standing near two motionless bodies on the ground. The officers pulled their guns on Russell and Georgiev, frisked them, and took Russell's notebook and one of Georgiev's cameras. Neither Russell nor Georgiev can determine if the two men were dead or alive. No police reports were ever filed about the incident. But the officers failed to take the memory card from Georgiev's camera and in December 2009, The Times-Picayune published the photos, hoping to determine what happened to the two men.

In August 2010, Russell tracks down the men in the photographs, Robert Williams and Ernest "Ricky" Bell. Both were alive and alleged that the police beat them after mistaking them for participants in a shootout. On Aug. 14, 2010, the Justice Department opened a civil rights investigation into the case.

September 1, 2005 Keenon McCann Shot by Police

Police receive reports of a man driving a stolen Kentwood Springs truck. The man attacked and robbed civilians when they approached the truck for water. A group of officers zero in on several parked trucks; New Orleans resident Keenon McCann is standing near them, reportedly holding a gun. The group opened fire and shot McCann; but upon arresting him, no weapon was found. Two of the officers involved, Captain Jeff Winn and Lieutenant Dwayne Scheuermann, both claimed that they were in serious danger at the time of the shooting. A friend of McCann claimed that the reports of him being armed were bogus.

McCann was arrested but released on his own recognizance. He was never charged with a crime and later filed a civil lawsuit against the NOPD. McCann was murdered in August 2008 with the lawsuit pending. No one has been charged in his death. Federal investigators are now looking into the circumstances surrounding his 2005 shooting.

September 2, 2005 "These Troops Know How to Shoot and Kill..."

Louisiana Governor Kathleen Blanco brings in 300 Arkansas National Guard troops to help restore order. She stated, "They have M-16s and they are locked and loaded. ... These troops know how to shoot and kill and they are more than willing to do so if necessary and I expect they will".

Governor Blanco went on to say, "What we were doing was strengthening the appearance of a lawful environment. Everybody here had now gotten very fearful, whether it was justified or not. I just decided that we needed to make a very dramatic statement to calm the media down and to calm the citizenry down."

September 2, 2005 Henry Glover Shot and Killed

Glover was allegedly shot by a police officer near an Algiers strip mall where he and a friend, Bernard Calloway, were picking up stolen goods. Glover's brother, Edward King, was called to the scene. King waves down a motorist, William Tanner.

Tanner drives Glover and King to a makeshift police station at Habans Elementary School. Tanner and King claimed that upon arriving, they were handcuffed and assaulted. Tanner's car, with Glover still inside, was driven away by police. Glover is never again seen alive.

A burned car containing Glover's badly charred body was discovered on a levee by two private security consultants about a week after Hurricane Katrina. One of the men, Istvan Balogh, reported his findings to federal authorities, the NOPD, the state police, and the military. Another week goes by before Glover's remains are taken to the coroner's office. In his final report, Coroner Frank Minyard, leaves the cause of death blank and the case is set aside. Eight months later,

Glover's remains were identified through DNA evidence and returned to his family.

Depiction of Scene in the Case of Henry Glover

DETAILS OF THE GLOVER CASE

Federal investigators are looking into the circumstances surrounding the Algiers shooting of 31-year-old Henry Glover on Sept. 2, 2005. Sources have said the FBI is investigating whether NOPD officers were responsible for shooting Glover and later burning his body.

1 A police report about a shooting that matches the details from the Glover case claims two men exited a white pick up truck and ran toward the rear gate of a strip mall on Gen. De Gaulle Drive.

2 NOPD officers David Warren and Linda Howard were stationed on the second-floor balcony of a building where the 4th District's detective bureau was located. Their exact locations are not clear from the police report. Warren stated that he fired at one of the men after seeing an object in his hand that Warren "perceived as a weapon."

3 The report states that the men fled on foot on Seine Street, leaving their truck behind. Although the report does not say what direction the men headed in, the injured Glover was picked up by a stranger, William Tanner, near the intersection of Seine Street and Texas Drive.

4 Tanner, along with Glover's brother and another man, took the injured man in his Chevrolet Malibu to Paul B. Habans Elementary School, which was the temporary headquarters of the NOPD SWAT team at the time, after Hurricane Katrina.

Tanner said officers were abusive and didn't help Glover.

5 Eventually, Tanner said an officer drove off in his Malibu, with Glover still in the back seat.

The car was later found in a ravine on the levee near Patterson Drive and Gen. Collins Avenue.

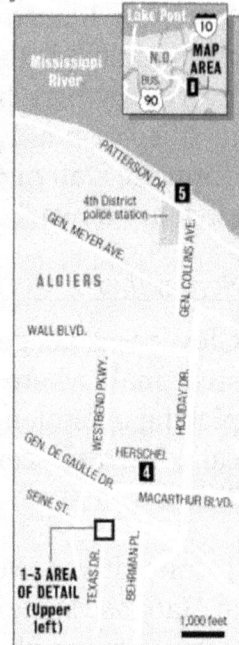

Source: Staff research
THE TIMES-PICAYUNE

On Dec. 18, 2008, ProPublica reporter A.C. Thompson's article on the Glover case, was published in The Nation. U.S. Attorney Jim Letten launched an investigation after media reports. The FBI began investigating Glover's death as a possible civil rights violation.

On June 11, 2010, former Officer David Warren was charged with shooting and killing Glover. Four other officers were indicted for their roles in the incident. Lieutenant Dwayne Scheuermann and Officer Greg McRae were charged with assaulting Tanner and King, burning the car containing Glover's body, and obstructing a federal investigation. Former Lieutenant Robert Italiano and Lieutenant Travis McCabe were charged with obstructing justice and lying to the FBI. McCabe was also charged with perjury.

September 3, 2005 Matthew McDonald Shot and Killed By Police

McDonald, a 41 year old drifter who had recently moved to New Orleans from Connecticut, was shot in the back and killed after allegedly threatening officers with a gun and refusing to drop his weapon.

Matthew McDonald's family in Connecticut received several conflicting accounts of his death. It was not until they were contacted by a reporter in late 2009 that they even learned he had been shot by a police officer. As of August 2010, a federal grand jury has been investigating the case.

September 3, 2005 Danny Brumfield, Sr. Shot and Killed Outside Convention Center

Officer Ronald Mitchell and his partner, Officer Ray Jones, claimed that Danny Brumfield was waving something shiny in his left hand. He ran toward their police vehicle and jumped on the hood. Mitchell says his feared for his life and shot Brumfield, killing him. Brumfield's family asserted that he was trying to wave down help when the police vehicle accelerated into him.

Brumfield's family filed a wrongful death lawsuit against the city of New Orleans. They were awarded $400,000 in July

2008. In August 2010, Mitchell and Jones received letters informing them that they were targets in a federal investigation of Brumfield's death.

September 4, 2005 Shooting on the Danziger Bridge

Police received a distress call indicating that members of the NOPD were being shot at on the Danziger Bridge. Several officers piled into a Budget rental truck, drove to the scene, and opened fire. Six civilians were shot; two of them, James Brissette and Ronald Madison, died from their injuries.

In December 2006, the New Orleans District Attorney's office indicted seven officers in the shootings. Judge Raymond Bigelow dismissed the charges in October 2008 due to prosecutorial missteps. U.S. Attorney Jim Letten announced the start of a federal investigation a month later. After an exhaustive inquiry, the feds alleged that the civilians on the bridge were unarmed and that police concocted a massive conspiracy to cover up their actions.

Eleven officers were indicted for their roles in the incident. Sgt. Kenneth Bowen, Sgt. Robert Gisevius, former Officer Robert Faulcon, and Officer Anthony Villavaso were each charged with a civil rights violation in the shooting death of Brisette. They were also charged with injuring several members of the Bartholomew family.

Faulcon and Bowen were also charged with civil rights violations in the death of Madison. Faulcon was charged with killing the mentally disabled man, who was shot in the back. Bowen was charged with kicking and stomping on Madison's body after he had been shot.

Homicide detectives Sgt. Arthur Kaufman and former Sgt. Gerard Dugue were charged, along with Bowen, Gisevius,

Faulcon, and Villavaso with participating in the cover-up, conspiracy to obstruct justice, and making false statements to investigators.

Five additional current and former officers have pled guilty to various charges. Ignatius Hills plead guilty to one count of conspiracy, to obstruct justice, and to one count of misprision of a felony, or failing to report a crime. Michael Hunter plead guilty to one count of conspiring to obstruct justice and to one count of misprision of a felony. Robert Barrios plead guilty to one count of conspiracy to obstruct justice. Michael Lohman plead guilty to obstructing justice. Jeffrey Lehrmann plead guilty to misprison of a felony.

September 27, 2005 Chief Compass Resigns

Chief Eddie Compass resigned and was replaced by second-in-command, Warren Riley. At the time, the department was under heavy scrutiny over leadership failures and allegations of officers abandoning their posts during the hurricane.

February 2010 A New Mayor, a New Chief of Police

In February, Mitch Landrieu was elected mayor. He appointed Nashville Police Chief, Ronal Serpas. Serpas, a former NOPD Deputy Superintendent, was second-in-command to lead the department under Richard Pennington. Critics hoped that Serpas, having served under Pennington and with experience outside of New Orleans, could help reform the troubled department.

*Summer 2010 U.S. Justice Department brought into New
Orleans; indictments in post-Katrina shootings*

On May 5, Mayor Landrieu sent a letter to U.S. Attorney
General Eric Holder, asking for his support and partnership
in transforming the New Orleans Police Department. He
stated that he had "inherited a police force that has been
described by many as one of the worst police departments in
the country".

In August, members of the Justice Department were
dispatched to New Orleans to investigate the city's police
department, root out corruption, and advise leaders on how
to improve the department's relationship with citizens.

As of August 25, more than a dozen current and former
officers were indicted. There are at least nine ongoing federal
investigations of the NOPD. Most of the investigations
involve actions taken by the police during the aftermath of
Hurricane Katrina.

Case Study on Local Government Consolidation

In the mid-1960s, the city of Jacksonville, Florida faced
complex urban problems and challenges. This included the
loss of accreditation for local high schools, the collapsing of
outdated infrastructure of sewage and road systems, heavily
polluted air from pulp mills and chemical plants, rampant
water pollution in the St. Johns River, numerous corruption
charges and grand jury indictments of public officials,
widespread areas of substandard housing, lack of
rudimentary city services to outlying areas, and high property
taxes vis-à-vis the quality of governmental services.

Multiple governmental structures, including a City Commission, City Council, County Budget Committee, and County Commission overlapped political jurisdictions which led to inefficient, costly, and duplicative services. In 1965, in an effort to ameliorate these problems, public and private leaders in Jacksonville made the first steps toward a merger of city and county governments.

In 1966, public officials established a local government study commission, called "Blueprint for Improvement". They also implanted a charter which paved the way for a special referendum held on August 8, 1967. The referendum ushered in a transitional planning period of just over a year to prepare for the official establishment of the new government (UNF, 2008).

Consolidation of governmental services, specifically law enforcement services, is often debated over two primary issues; a cost savings verses a political preference to maintain local control of services. Most Americans are likely to accept a government consolidation initiated within the states and local governments. However, they adamantly oppose a federal government consolidation.

※

CHAPTER 6 - INTERNATIONAL LAW ENFORCEMENT ORGANIZATIONAL COMPARISON

Canada

Canada is a constitutional Monarchy. This is a form of constitutional government in which a Monarch is the head of state. The head of the Canadian government is an elected Prime Minister. Elizabeth II, Queen of Canada, is the sovereign and head of state of Canada (Canada FAQ, 2011).

CANADIAN GOVERNMENT

Canada is also a Parliamentary democracy. The Parliament of Canada is located in the Canadian capital of Ottawa. It is formed by three major entities; the sovereign of Canada, the Canadian Senate, and the Canadian House of Commons. The Canadian Senate has 105 members appointed by the Governor General of Canada (on behalf of the sovereign).

The Canadian House of Commons has 308 seats and the Canadian people directly elect the House of Commons members. The House of Commons is the most important part of the Canadian Parliament. The Canadian Prime Minister and Cabinet must have the support of a majority of members of the House of Commons to remain in power (Canada FAQ, 2011).

Canada is made up of 10 provinces and three territories, making it a Federation. The Ministry of Public Safety is Canada's lead department for public safety. Public Safety Canada works with five agencies and three review bodies. They are united in a single portfolio and report to the same minister. The result is better integration among federal organizations dealing with national security, emergency management, law enforcement, corrections, crime prevention, and borders.

Together, these agencies have an annual budget of $6 billion and more than 52,000 employees working in every part of the country.

AGENCIES

CANADA PUBLIC SAFETY PORTFOLIO
Canadian Public Safety and National Police Organization

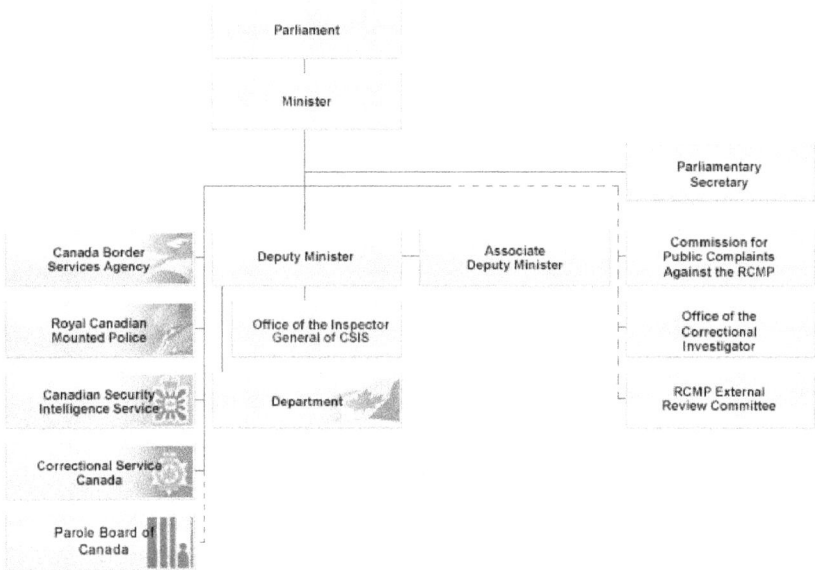

Parliament

Minister

Parliamentary Secretary

Canada Border Services Agency

Deputy Minister

Associate Deputy Minister

Commission for Public Complaints Against the RCMP

Royal Canadian Mounted Police

Office of the Inspector General of CSIS

Office of the Correctional Investigator

Canadian Security Intelligence Service

Department

RCMP External Review Committee

Correctional Service Canada

Parole Board of Canada

The Canada Border Services Agency (CBSA) manages the nation's borders by enforcing Canadian laws governing trade and travel, as well as international agreements and conventions. CBSA facilitates legitimate cross-border traffic and supports economic development while stopping people and goods that pose a potential threat to Canada.

The Canadian Security Intelligence Service (CSIS) investigates and reports on activities that may pose a threat to the security of Canada. The CSIS also provides security assessments on request to all federal departments and agencies.

The Correctional Service Canada (CSC) helps protect society by encouraging offenders to become law-abiding citizens while exercising reasonable, safe, secure, and humane control. The CSC is responsible for managing offenders sentenced to two years or more in federal correctional institutions and under community supervision.

The Parole Board of Canada (PBC) is an independent decision making body that grants, denies, or revokes parole for inmates in federal prisons. The NPB helps protect society by facilitating the timely reintegration of offenders into society as law-abiding citizens. The Board also makes conditional release (parole) decisions for provincial inmates in provinces without their own parole board.

The Royal Canadian Mounted Police (RCMP) enforces Canadian laws, prevents crime and maintains peace, order and security. This includes preventing, detecting, and investigating offences against federal statutes. In provinces, territories, and municipalities where the RCMP has a policing contract, it maintains law and order and prevents, detects, and investigates crime. This institution also provides investigative and protective services to other federal departments and agencies. Additionally, the RCMP provides Canadian and international law enforcement agencies with specialized police training and research, forensic laboratory services, identification services, and informatics technology.

OVERSIGHT/REVIEW AUTHORITY

The Commission for Public Complaints against the RCMP (CPC) receives complaints from the public about the conduct of members of the RCMP. It reviews and investigates these complaints in an open, independent, and objective manner. The Commission also holds public hearings and conducts research and policy development to improve the public complaint process.

The Office of the Correctional Investigator (OCI) conducts independent, thorough and timely investigations about issues related to Correctional Service Canada that affect offenders either individually or as a group. The OCI may initiate an investigation based on a complaint from (or on behalf of) an offender, at the request of the Minister of Public Safety, or on its own initiative.

The RCMP External Review Committee (ERC) is an independent agency that promotes fair and equitable labor relations within the RCMP. The Committee conducts an independent review of appeals in disciplinary, discharge and demotion matters, as well as certain kinds of grievances.

In addition to providing policing services to all Canadians nationally, the RCMP also delivers services under contract to the three territories, eight provinces (except Ontario and Quebec), nearly 200 municipalities, and nearly 200 First Nations communities (RCMP, 2011).

Ontario, Quebec, Newfoundland, and Labrador maintain their own provincial police forces: the Ontario Provincial Police, Sûreté du Québec (Quebec Provincial Police), and Royal Newfoundland Constabulary. Smaller municipalities often contract police service from the provincial policing authority, while larger ones maintain their own force. Newfoundland's provincial police force is only responsible for its larger urban areas. The province has contracted the RCMP to patrol the rest of the province. The RCMP, colloquially known as *Mounties*, is the only police force to service all three levels in some areas of the country (UAA, 2011).

There are also a few private police forces with some of the powers usually reserved for governmental forces (as it relates to company property). The Canadian National Railway and Canadian Pacific Railway each have their own police force. Any railway in Canada can appoint police officers. Some private hospitals and universities also employ private special police as well as quasi government agencies such as transit commissions and power authorities. The duties of private railway police are to prevent crimes against the company, protection of goods, materials and public rail transit being moved on their rail systems. They work to protect the public, rail personnel, and property that is owned or administered by the railways (UAA, 2011).

The regular public police maintain authority and jurisdiction for all criminal offenses, regardless of the offense occurring on public or private property. A local police chief has legislated and common law authority as the police of responsibility for territory under his command. Private police do not have legislated duties and are not legally obligated to maintain or police their property with private police officers.

All taxpayers, companies, and citizens have equal access to public police. Many companies and quasi government agencies find that it is cost efficient and reduces liability to have security or sworn special police. Thus, a company can direct its resources to matters that it finds important and control its own private interests (RCMP, 2011).

The RCMP is organized into a more regional management system under the direction of deputy commissioners. The four regions include Pacific, Northwestern, Central, and Atlantic. According to the Canadian government, this construct ensures a greater grass-roots involvement in decision-making and also allows the RCMP to invest more resources into frontline services.

Under the Commissioner, operational direction is provided by Deputy Commissioners in charge of:

- Federal Services and Central Region (Ottawa)

- Operations and Integration

- National Police Services

- Corporate Management and Comptrollership

- Atlantic Region (Halifax)

- North West Region (Regina)

- Pacific Region (Vancouver)

Total Force Strength for all Police in Canada: +65,000

CANADA CRIME STATISTICS BY PROVINCE AND TERRITORY

Crime statistics vary considerably through different parts of Canada. In general, the eastern provinces have the lowest violent crime rates while the western provinces have higher rates and the territories higher still. Of all the provinces, Saskatchewan has the highest violent crime rate.

2006 crime statistics for the provinces and territories are given below, as reported by Statistics Canada (last updated: February 28, 2007).

Crimes Rates By Offenses For Each Province And Territory, 2006

	Canada	N.L	P.E.I	N.S.	N.B.	Qu.	Ont.	Man.	Sask.	Alta.	B.C.	Y.T.	N.W.T	Nvt.
	rate per 100,000 population													
All incidents	8,269	6,571	7,486	8,698	6,781	6,626	6,251	12,325	15,276	10,336	12,564	22,197	44,074	32,831
Criminal Code offences (excluding traffic offenses)	7,519	6,055	6,793	8,069	6,111	5,909	5,689	11,679	13,711	9,523	11,365	20,593	41,468	31,265
Crimes of violence	951	851	714	1,135	849	756	756	1,598	2,039	1,101	1,218	3,007	6,448	6,764
Homicide	1.9	1.4	0.7	1.7	0.9	1.2	1.5	3.3	4.1	2.8	2.5	0.0	0.0	6.5
Attempted murder	2.6	1.0	0.7	3.0	1.2	3.3	2.5	2.2	4.7	2.3	2.1	0.0	0.0	13.0
Assaults (level 1 to 3)	735	734	625	919	706	540	563	1,243	1,671	888	980	2,655	5,834	5,893
Sexual assault	68	67	48	86	67	67	56	108	125	64	75	195	373	598
Other sexual offences	9	5	11	7	18	13	5	11	15	7	10	51	55	46
Robbery	94	23	17	85	30	91	87	182	150	93	110	58	36	39
Other crimes of violence	41	20	12	34	27	40	41	48	71	44	39	48	151	169
Property crimes	3,588	2,363	3,000	3,514	2,562	3,114	2,811	4,951	4,776	4,480	5,685	5,107	6,357	4,256
Breaking &entering	768	737	537	735	599	867	541	1,074	1,228	768	1,088	1,467	2,332	1,965
Motor vehicle theft	487	131	115	263	187	507	303	1,376	633	725	682	445	927	621
Theft over $5,000	52	15	31	44	38	65	44	49	42	66	58	61	65	36
Theft $5,000 & under	1,889	1,252	2,002	1,940	1,446	1,399	1,531	2,152	2,392	2,383	3,367	2,780	2,654	1,316
Possession of stolen goods	108	34	52	233	54	43	110	88	160	188	139	77	136	140
Frauds	284	195	263	299	239	234	283	214	320	350	351	279	244	179

Continue On Next Page

(CONTINUED) Crimes Rates By Offenses

Other Criminal Code offenses	2,980	2,841	3,079	3,420	2,700	2,039	2,122	5,130	6,896	3,942	4,462	12,479	28,664	20,246
Criminal Code offences (traffic offences)	368	279	508	328	321	415	245	284	963	490	441	974	1,393	809
Impaired driving	228	221	396	255	242	214	139	213	474	347	340	701	1,168	686
Other c.c. traffic offences	140	59	112	74	79	201	106	71	489	144	101	272	225	124
Federal statutes	383	237	186	301	349	302	317	362	602	322	758	631	1,214	757
Drugs	295	128	127	218	248	266	239	183	275	258	617	468	769	673
Other federal statutes	88	109	59	83	102	36	79	179	327	64	141	163	444	85

DIFFERENCES BETWEEN US POLICE AND CANADIAN POLICE SYSTEMS

The most notable difference is in the way power and authority functionally operates between the two countries. For example, in the US, prosecutors act in the name of "the people" whereas Canadian prosecutors act in the name of "the Crown." Although it is an independent nation, Canadians chooses to have the British Queen as their sovereign.

Thus, the famous opening line of *Law and Order* would have to be translated to "In the criminal justice system, the Crown is represented by two separate yet equally important groups: the Mounted Police who investigate crime and the Public Prosecutors who prosecute the offenders". A 'peace officer' has jurisdiction across the entire country, although the police are generally assigned to specific areas. Legally, they can act as police anywhere in the country.

In the U.S., authority is derived from either the state (sovereign) or the federal government as prescribed in the Constitution. For example, the people in the homeland (city, county, and state) can elect or appoint the police and generally empower them to enforce laws within the respective jurisdiction of the governing body. There are cooperative agreements which allow limited excursions across different jurisdictional boundaries. They have no authority to enforce laws outside their jurisdiction.

However, federal law enforcement officers have jurisdiction anywhere in the U.S. and jurisdiction of the federal government. This includes the FBI, the U.S. Secret Service, and the U.S. Marshals Service and Drug Enforcement Administration.

The RCMP jurisdiction is similar to the FBI. Newfoundland has the Royal Newfoundland Constabulary. This is more than the city, but does not cover the entire province. The U.S. public police are more diverse and organized based on jurisdiction.

Russia

RUSSIAN GOVERNMENT

Type: Federation
Independence: August 24, 1991
Constitution: December 12, 1993

Branches:

- Executive - President, Prime Minister (chairman of the government)

- Legislative - Federal Assembly (Federation Council, State Duma)

- Judicial - Constitutional Court, Supreme Court, Supreme Court of Arbitration, and Office of Procurator General

After a shakeup in late 2008, several political parties were dissolved and combined, leaving seven registered parties. The remaining registered parties include United Russia, the Communist Party (KPRF), the Liberal Democratic Party (LDPR), Just Russia, Yabloko, Patriots of Russia, and the new Right Cause Party. Yabloko, favoring liberal reforms and Patriots of Russia, failed to clear the 7% threshold in 2007 to enter the Duma (DOS, 2011).

There are 83 federal subjects (members of the Federation) which include 21 republics, 9 krays, 46 oblasts, 2 federal cities, one autonomous oblast, and four autonomous okrugs. Voting is universal at 18 years of age.

In the political system established by the 1993 constitution, the President wields considerable executive power. There is no Vice President and the Legislative Branch is far weaker than the Executive. The bicameral legislature consists of the Lower House (State Duma) and the Upper House (the Federation Council).

The President nominates the highest state officials, including the Prime Minister, who must also be approved by the Duma. However, the President can pass decrees without consent from the Duma. He also is head of the armed forces and of the Security Council (DOS, 2011).

Dmitriy Medvedev, running as United Russia's candidate, was elected to a four-year term as President on March 2, 2008, with 70.28% of the vote. The Russian constitution does not allow Presidents to serve more than two consecutive terms. A December 2008 law extended the terms of Duma Deputies from four to five years and Presidential terms from four to six years. The new terms take effect with the next elections, which for the Duma are scheduled to occur in December 2011 and for President in March 2012 (DOS, 2011).

Russia is a Federation. However, the precise distribution of powers between the central government and the regional and local authorities is still evolving. The Russian Federation consists of 84 administrative units, including two federal cities of Moscow and St. Petersburg. The constitution explicitly defines the federal government's exclusive powers. It also describes most key regional issues as the joint responsibility of the federal government and the regional administrative units.

In 2000, President Vladimir Putin grouped the regions into seven federal districts with Presidential appointees established in Moscow and six provincial capitals. In March 2004, the Constitution was amended to permit the merger of some regional administrative units. A law enacted in December 2004 eliminated the direct election of the country's regional leaders. Governors are now nominated by the President and subject to confirmation by regional legislatures (DOS, 2011).

The Police *(Politsiya)* are the central law enforcement body in Russia, operating under the Ministry of Internal Affairs. The new agency was established in 2011 to replace the Militsiya (militia), the former police service. This reorganization was initiated by the Russian Federation President, Dmitry Medvedev in order to reform the police agencies. The police in Russia have a long history of brutality and corruption (RMOI, 2011). The Russian Police operates according to the Law on Police, which has been approved by the Federal Assembly and subsequently signed into law on February 7, 2011 by President Medvedev (LOC, 2011).

The Bill on Police established a new law enforcement agency with the pre-1917 name. It was introduced by President Medvedev to the State Duma on October 27, 2010 as a part of the reforming process of the Ministry of Internal Affairs. The State Duma adopted the bill in the final reading on January 28, 2011 by a vote of 315–130.

It received the support of United Russia representatives only. The Federation Council approved it on February 2 by a vote 134–0, with 2 senators abstaining in the vote. This included Chairman of the Federation Council Sergey Mironov. The bill was signed into law by the President on February 7, 2011, taking effect on March 1, 2011 (LOC, 2011).

Law enforcement in Russia is the responsibility of a variety of different agencies. The Police (formerly Militsiya) are the civil police service of the Ministry of Internal Affairs. The Internal Troops provide a gendarmerie function, supporting the Police and dealing with large-scale riots and internal armed conflicts. They also provide security for highly-important facilities such as nuclear power plants.

The Federal Protective Service of Russia is responsible for the protection of Russian state property and high-ranking government personnel, including the President of Russia. In addition, the Ministry of Russia for Civil Defense and Emergencies and Elimination of Consequences of Natural Disasters is responsible for the civil defense regulation and protection from fire. It also has its own troops. The Federal Security Service (FSB) is the domestic security service and the main successor agency of the Soviet-era Cheka (State Political Directorate), NKVD (The People's Commiserate for Internal Affairs), and KGB (Committee for State Security). The Federal Border Guard Service is subordinate to the FSB.

Total Police Strength in Russia: 1,200,000 (approximate)

Budget: +$5 billion

In 2009, Russia was one of many countries hit hard by the global financial crisis. The economy shrank by about 8%. According to official statistics, the contemporaneous trends for crime shows a mixed picture. Overall crime actually decreased by 6.7% year-on-year, while economic crime increased almost eight-fold. A report from the interior-ministry's investigative committee found that 429,000 economic crimes had been uncovered. Of these crimes, 172,800 of them were deemed especially serious. Exposed instances of bribery rose by 13% and the cost of economic crime was accounted at an astounding $33 billion (Slade, 2010).

Moscow's 1995 statistics included 93,560 crimes, of which 18,500 were white-collar crimes. This was an increase of 8.3% from 1994. Among white-collar crimes in 1995, swindling increased 67.2% and extortion 37.5%. Among the conventional crimes reported, murder and attempted murder increased 1.5%, rape 6.5%, burglaries 6.6%, burglaries accompanied by violence 20.8%, and serious crimes by teenagers 2.2% (LOC, 1996).

The rate of crime-solving by the Moscow militia (police) rose in 1995 from 57.7% to 64.9%. However, that statistic was bolstered substantially by success in solving minor crimes. The projected rate of solving burglaries was 18.8%, murders 42.2%, and crimes involving use of a firearm 31.4%. Moscow and St. Petersburg were the centers of automobile theft, which increased dramatically through the first half of the 1990s (LOC, 1996).

In Moscow an estimated 50 cars were stolen per day. The estimated yearly total for Russia were between 100,000 and 150,000. In the first quarter of 1994, Russia averaged 84 murders a day. Many of those crimes were contract killings attributed to criminal organizations. In 1994, murder victims included three deputies of the State Duma, one journalist, a priest, the head of a union, several local officials, and more than 30 business-people and bankers. Most of these crimes went unsolved (LOC, 1996).

The 1995 national crime total exceeded 1.3 million, including 30,600 murders. Also in 1995, some 248 regular militia officers were killed in the line of duty (LOC, 1996).

Possession of firearms has been identified as another grave social problem. Confiscation of firearms increased substantially in 1995, according to the Moscow militia's Regional Organized Crime Directorate. About 3 million firearms were registered in 1995, but the number of unregistered guns was assumed to far exceed that figure.

Military weapons are stolen frequently and sold to gangsters. In 1993, nearly 60,000 cases of such theft were reported. This involved machine guns, hand grenades, and explosives. The ready availability of firearms has made the work of the poorly armed militia more dangerous (LOC, 1996).

Fundamentals of Russian police activity

Policy

- Observation of and respect for human and civil rights and freedoms
- Legality
- Impartiality
- Openness and transparency
- Public trust and the support of the citizens
- Interaction and cooperation with other law enforcement bodies, agencies, and citizens
- Use of scientific achievement, advanced technological and information systems

Priority tasks

- Fighting terrorism
- Fighting extremism
- Fighting organized crime
- Fighting corruption
- Development of a "Uniform Information and Telecommunications System" and "Safe City" comprehensive system

Form and content

- New uniforms for police officers will be designed by 2012
- Police personnel will be downsized by 20%. Only those who pass recertification will keep their jobs
- Monthly pay for police officers will amount to no less than 33,000 roubles ($1,100)

Police activities will be under control

- President, Chambers of the Federal Assembly, the government of the Russian Federation
- Citizens and public associations, Public Chamber of the Russian Federation, public supervisory commissions, public councils
- Judicial bodies
- Procurator-General and authorized procurators

RIANOVOSTI © 2011   www.rian.ru

Italy

ITALIAN GOVERNMENT

Type: Republic since June 2, 1946
Constitution: January 1, 1948

Branches:

- Executive - President (Chief of State), Council of Ministers (cabinet) headed by the President of the Council (Prime Minister)

- Legislative - Bicameral Parliament: 630-member Chamber of Deputies, 315-member Senate (plus a varying number of "life" Senators)

- Judicial - Independent Constitutional Court and Lower Magistracy

Subdivisions are made up of 94 provinces and 20 regions. The political parties include People of Liberty, Democratic Party, Northern League, Italy of Values, Union of the Center, and Movement for Autonomy. Vote for House is universal over 18 and vote for Senate is universal over 25. Italy has been a democratic republic since June 2, 1946, when the monarchy was abolished by popular referendum. The constitution was promulgated on January 1, 1948 (DOS, 2011).

The Italian state is centralized. The Prefect of each of the provinces is appointed by and answerable to the central government. In addition to the provinces, the constitution provides for 20 regions with limited governing powers. Five of the regions include Sardinia, Sicily, Trentino-Alto Adige, Valle d'Aosta and Friuli-Venezia Giulia. Each function with special autonomy statutes. The other 15 regions were established in 1970 and vote for regional "councils".

The establishment of regional governments throughout Italy has brought some decentralization to the national governmental machinery. Recent governments have also devolved further powers to the regions.

Many regional governments, particularly in the north of Italy, are seeking additional powers (DOS, 2011).

The 1948 constitution established a Bicameral Parliament (Chamber of Deputies and Senate), a separate judiciary, and an executive branch composed of a Council of Ministers (cabinet) that is headed by the President of the Council (Prime Minister). The President of the Republic is elected for seven years by the parliament sitting jointly with a small number of regional delegates. The President nominates the Prime Minister, who in turn, chooses the other ministers. The Council of Ministers, which is composed mostly of members of Parliament, must retain the confidence of both houses (DOS, 2011).

The Houses of Parliament are popularly and directly elected by a proportional representation system. Under 2005 legislation, the Chamber of Deputies has 630 members (12 of whom are elected by Italians abroad). In addition to 315 elected members (six of whom are elected by Italians abroad), the Senate includes former Presidents, and several other persons appointed for life according to special constitutional provisions. Both houses are elected for a maximum of five years, but either may be dissolved before the expiration of its normal term. Legislative bills may originate in either house and must be passed by a majority in both (DOS, 2011).

The Italian judicial system is based on Roman law modified by the Napoleonic code and subsequent statutes. There is only partial judicial review of legislation in the American sense. A constitutional court, which passes on the constitutionality of laws, is a post-World War II innovation.

Its powers and the volume and frequency of its decisions are not as extensive as those of the U.S. Supreme Court (DOS, 2011).

The headquarters of the National Police (Polizia di Stato or Polizia Statale) is located in Rome. There are regional and provincial divisions throughout Italy. This is a civil police service, contrast to the other police services in Italy (OSCE, 2011).

The National Police provides general police services in Italy. This includes patrolling of highways, railways and certain waterways, as well as assisting the local police. Every major Italian town or city has a main police station (Questura) run by the National Police (OSCE, 2011).

The Minister of the Interior is the national authority responsible for public order and security maintenance. In this capacity, the Minister is supported by the Public Order and Security Committee. This is an advisory body consisting of the Chief of Police (Director General of Public Security) and the heads of the other police services. Public Security Administration is exercised at central level by the Public Security Department, provincial and local authorities, and public security officials and officers at the local level.

The Public Security Department is headed by a Prefect. The rank of Police Chief is appointed by the President of the Republic based on proposals from the Minister of the Interior and by decision of the Council of Ministers. Tasks of the Public Security Department include implementing public order and security policy, ensuring technical and operational co-ordination and harmonization of police services, managing the National Police, and providing technical support for the Ministry's overall needs.

Provincial authorities include the Prefect, who is in charge of the Territorial Government Office and responsible for public order and security. Another provincial authority is the Questore. This is a senior National Police official responsible for the management and coordination of services and police force employment. Other special units include mobile units, bomb technicians, sharpshooters, a canine unit, the mounted police, air service, and nautical squads.

Another important operational sector of the National Police is represented by the specialties. About 24,000 staff, which is almost a quarter of the police personnel, works within several other services. This includes Traffic Police, Railway Police, Postal and Telecommunications Police, Border and Immigration Police.

In 2006, the number of Italian National Police personnel carrying out police functions amounted to approximately 110,000 persons with an additional 5,700 officers carrying out duties of a technical/scientific or purely technical nature (OSCE, 2011). Law enforcement in Italy is provided by eight separate police forces; six of which are National groups in Italy.

- **National Police Forces**

    - **Arma dei Carabinieri** (a Gendarmerie-like military corps with police duties that also serves as the Italian military police)

    - **Guardia di Finanza** (a corps of the Italian Army under the authority of the Minister of Economy and Finance with a role as police force. It is in charge of financial, economic, judiciary and public safety, tax evasion, financial crimes, smuggling, money laundering, international illegal drug trafficking, illegal immigration, customs and borders checks, copyright violations, anti-Mafia operations, credit card fraud, cybercrime, counterfeiting, terrorist financing, maintaining public order, and safety, political and military defense of the Italian border)

-   **Polizia di Stato** (State Police is the civil national police of Italy responsible for patrolling, investigative and law enforcement duties, patrolling the Autostrada which is Italy's Express Highway network, and oversees the security of railways, bridges and waterways)

-   **Polizia Penitenziaria** (Prison Guards, literally Penitentiary Police, operates the Italian prison system and handles the transportation of inmates)

-   **Corpo Forestale dello Stato** (National Forestry Department is responsible for law enforcement in Italian national parks and forests. Their duties include enforcing poaching laws, safeguarding protected animal species, and preventing forest fires. A recent law reform expanded its duties to food controls. In Italy it has the responsibility to manage the activities related to the Convention on International Trade in Endangered Species)

-   **Coast Guard** (under the control of the Ministry of Infrastructure and Transport, provides law enforcement on the sea and is part of the Italian Navy)

- **Local police forces**

    - **Provincial Police** (operate in only some of the 109 provinces of Italy. Their main duties are to enforce regional and national hunting and fishing laws. They have also expanded into wildlife management and environmental protection)

    - **Municipal Police** (main duty is to enforce local regulations, control traffic, and handle petty crime and anti-social behavior in the largest metropolitan areas. These forces can be called Polizia Municipale, Polizia Locale, Polizia Comunale, Polizia Urbana or *Vigili Urbani*. In some regions Polizia Provinciale and Polizia Municipale are grouped into the *Polizia Locale* name, although they keep their own internal organization. Smaller communes can merge their local police forces in a consortium)

Total active Police Forces - +324,339

Criminality levels, which have been rising since 1991, have continued to fluctuate over time. However, it still retains fairly stable levels. In 2008, a total of 2,709,888 crimes (4,529.1 per hundred thousand inhabitants) was recorded. This was a decrease of 7.6% from the previous year. Under the quantity profile, the decrease was caused in particular by accusations of theft. This, alone, represents more than half of the reported crimes (approximately 244,000, with a fall of 14.9% (OSCE, 2011).

Public Security Department

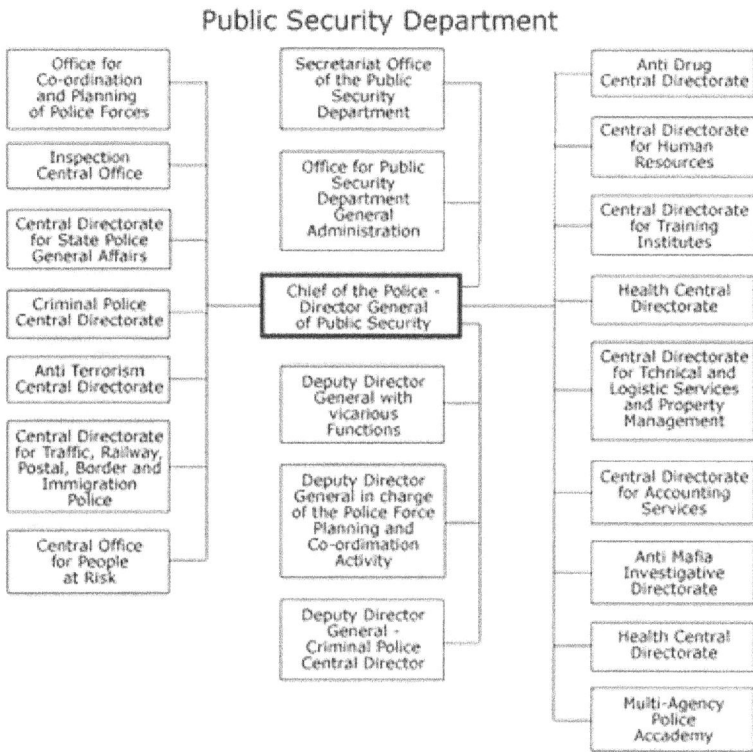

The Theoretical National Organization

How many active law enforcement agencies are operating in the U.S. today? How many sworn officers and agents would be needed to support a consolidated National Police Agency?

Local, State, Federal, Tribal and Campus Agencies in US (2008)

Police	Sheriff	State	Federal	Tribal Police	Campus PD
+11,766 Municipal Police Departments (2008)	+3,100 County Sheriff's Departments (2008)	26 Highway Patrol 23 State Police 1 Hawaii Department of Public Safety (2008)	65 Federal Law Enforcement Agencies (2008)	+200 Police Departments in 341 Recognized Tribes (2008)	+1,000 Public Police Departments (2008)
+700,000 Sworn Officers and Civilians (2008)	+330,274 Sworn Officers and Civilians (2008)	+107,803 Troopers, Highway Patrol and Civilians (2008)	+105,000 Sworn Agents/Officers and Civilians (Excluding DOD, USCG, CIA & TSA) (2008)	2380 Sworn Officers – 1,154 Non-Sworn Civilians (2008)	+25,000 Sworn Officers and Civilians (2008)
State Prisons	Tribal Facilities	Juvenile Detention Facilities	Federal Prisons	Jails	Private Correctional Facilities
1,350	69		115		158

(Breakdown of current Law Enforcement/Corrections Agencies in the US)

Based on published reports, there are more than 17,000 law enforcement agencies (municipal, metropolitan, county, campus, tribal and state police agencies and 65 federal law enforcement agencies) in the U.S. that are supported by approximately 1.1 million employees (sworn officers/agents and civilian employees). They serve a population of 310,017,004 people in 48 contiguous states, including Hawaii and Alaska. Other English-speaking democracies have a much smaller number such as Canada with 461, England with 43, India with 22, and Australia with 8.

An estimated $115 billion are spent every year on law enforcement and corrections. Many of the police agencies have overlapping jurisdictions at multiple levels of government. This includes city, town, township, county and parish, tribal, state, and federal agencies. The majority are general-purpose agencies that are responsible for patrolling a certain area, responding to calls from citizens, and investigating crimes.

Corrections costs have quadrupled in just the past 20 years and now account for 1 out of every 15 state general fund discretionary dollars. 36 Corrections has been the second fastest-growing category of state budgets. This is behind only Medicaid. Nearly 90% of this spending has gone to prisons (PEW, 2010).

Most local police departments in the U.S. are small. More than 11,000 employ fewer than 25 full-time sworn officers, over 5,700 employ fewer than 5 officers, and over 1,100 rely only on part-time officers. Others departments are special-purpose agencies that are responsible for a specific territory (San Diego Harbor Police responsible for the Unified Port of San Diego which includes San Diego International Airport) or function (Alcohol Beverage Control in Florida).

Some agencies do not fall neatly within these categories. In some states, sheriffs' agencies do not provide police patrol. However, they do provide a variety of other related services such as managing and operating jails, guarding courtrooms, providing canine services, undercover deputies, and investigative assistance to local police agencies. These variations in size, type, and function of American police agencies make it difficult to establish an ideal method of organization and management applicable to all agencies.

ORGANIZATION

Theoretical
National Defense and Enforcement

Federal Emergency Management Agency (FEMA)	Department of Defense (DOD)	Department of Homeland Security (DHS)	Department of National Police (DNP)	Department of National Intelligence (DNI)
National Emergency and Disaster Management	Homeland Defense U.S. NORTHCOM	Homeland Security	National Law Enforcement	Domestic and International Terrorism
	Air Defense	U.S. Coast Guard (USCG)		National Counterterrorism Center
	Border Security	Transportation Security Administration (TSA)		
	External Threats	Port Security		
		Rail Security		
		Domestic Nuclear Detection		
		Domestic Cyber Security		

Overview of National Defense and Law Enforcement Authority
(direct reports of the President)

A National Police Act (Constitutional Amendment) would have broad powers, concurrent jurisdiction (permits both state and federal governments to enforce/prosecute crimes), and exclusive authority to establish a central police organization. Included in the amendment would be the 48 contiguous states, Alaska, Hawaii, and U.S. territories.

The National Police Act would also establish Regional Police Bureaus (RPB) and Public Safety Commissions (PSC) in the Northern, Southern, Eastern, and Western Regions of the

U.S. (not necessarily aligned with District Courts or political districting). It would also grant authority to carry out police duties to protect life, person, and property. Also, it would maintain public safety and order within its jurisdiction.

The Public Safety Commissions, modeled after the National Commission, would establish oversight and administrative supervision over the police. Similar Commissions would also be established for the Bureau of Prisons. A consortium of governors from each respective region would nominate the Commissioners to the President, but would not have operational command and control over the police agencies.

Northern Region	Southern Region	Eastern Region	Western Region
Minnesota, North Dakota, South Dakota, Iowa, Illinois, Wisconsin, Michigan, Indiana, Kentucky, Ohio	Missouri, Arkansas, Tennessee, Louisiana, Mississippi, Georgia, Alabama, Florida, South Carolina, North Carolina	Virginia, West Virginia, District of Columbia, Pennsylvania, Maryland, Delaware, New Jersey, New York, Connecticut, New Hampshire, Rhode Island, Maine, Vermont, Massachusetts	Alaska, Hawaii, California, Washington, Oregon, Montana, Idaho, Wyoming, Utah, Nevada, Arizona, New Mexico, Texas, Colorado, Kansas, Nebraska,
		Puerto Rico	Guam
		US Virgin Islands	
		Guantanamo Bay, Cuba	

Notional Regional Police Bureaus and Territorial Jurisdictions

NATIONAL POLICE ORGANIZATION (NPO)

There are many national and international examples that can be used as models to organize a central agency. These examples include Jacksonville Sheriff's Office, Japan National Police, and the Italian Public Security – National Police. The uniqueness of law enforcement and sensitivity to civil liberties require special circumstances for oversight and uniformity. For this report, the U.S. National Police Organization would be a new department lead by a cabinet level Secretary (Policy Maker), National Public Safety Commission (Administrative Oversight), and the National Police Agency (Operational Authority).

United States National Police Organization

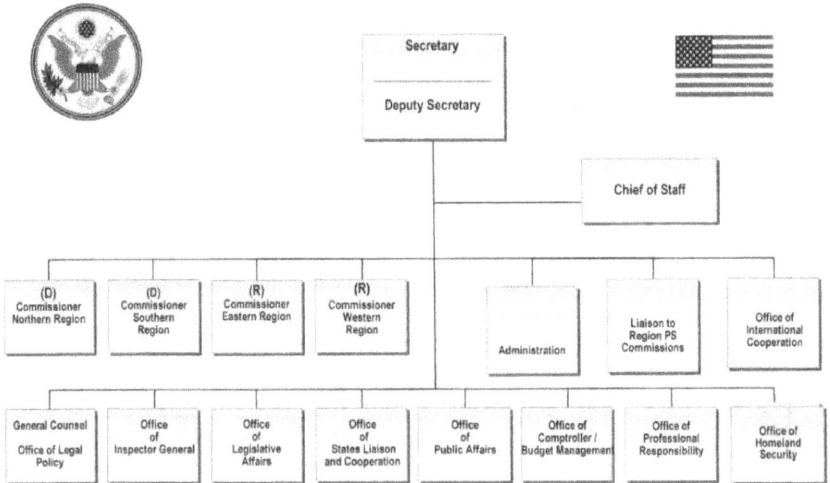

UNITED STATES DEPARTMENT OF NATIONAL POLICE (DNP)

The National Police Organization is a cabinet level department lead by the Secretary of the Department of National Police. The Secretary reports to the President of the United States on all matters of domestic law enforcement and police services within the jurisdiction of the federal government and in accordance with the National Police Act. The Secretary is nominated by the President and confirmed by the Senate.

NATIONAL PUBLIC SAFETY COMMISSION (NPSC)

The NPSC system would be established to ensure the democratic administration and political neutrality of police under the administrative supervision by the commission. The NPSC would consist of people with good standing in their communities that understand the importance of oversight and be of good moral character. The NPSC reports to the Secretary of National Police. The Commissioners are nominated by the President and confirmed by the Senate.

The NPSC would exercise administrative supervision over the National Police Agency (NPA). While the commission is under the jurisdiction of the President, the President is not involved in the day to day routines, nor would he be involved in direct command and control issues. This ensures the Commission's independence and political neutrality.

The NPSC formulates basic policies and regulations and coordinates police administration on matters of national concern. It also authorizes general standards for training, communications, criminal identification, criminal statistics, and equipment among other duties as required.

The NPSC nominates to the President the NPA Commandant. Deputy Commandant, the "G7" (Bureau of Prisons, Special Operations and Tactics, Bureau of Investigations and Counter-terrorism, Uniformed Police, National Training and Certifications, Human Resources and Police Support Services), and the Regional Police Bureau (RPB) Chiefs are appointed by the NPA.

Organizationally, the NPSC would comprise of a Chairman (Secretary of National Police - tie breaker vote only), Deputy Chairman (Under Secretary of National Police – non-voting), and four members (voting authority). Individual commissioners would serve a five year term. They would be appointed by the President and confirmed by the Senate. To ensure political neutrality, no more than two members may belong to the same political party. The Chairman would approve staffing and budgets for individual commissioners.

National Police Agency (NPA)
ORGANIZATION AND AUTHORITY

The Chief Executive Officer of the NPA would be a 5-Star Commandant nominated by the NPSC to the President and confirmed by the Senate. The Commandant, under the administrative supervision of the NPSC, administers the agency's operations, appoints and dismisses agency employees, and supervises and controls the RPBs within the agency's defined duties. Mandatory requirement include a law enforcement background and service as a Chief of Police (major city, e.g.,, New York, Philadelphia or Los Angeles), Sheriff (major county, e.g.,, Los Angeles County, San Diego County, King County or Shelby County), Director (state police), or Director (major federal law enforcement agency - FBI, Marshals Service or Secret Service).

US National Police Agency (NPA)

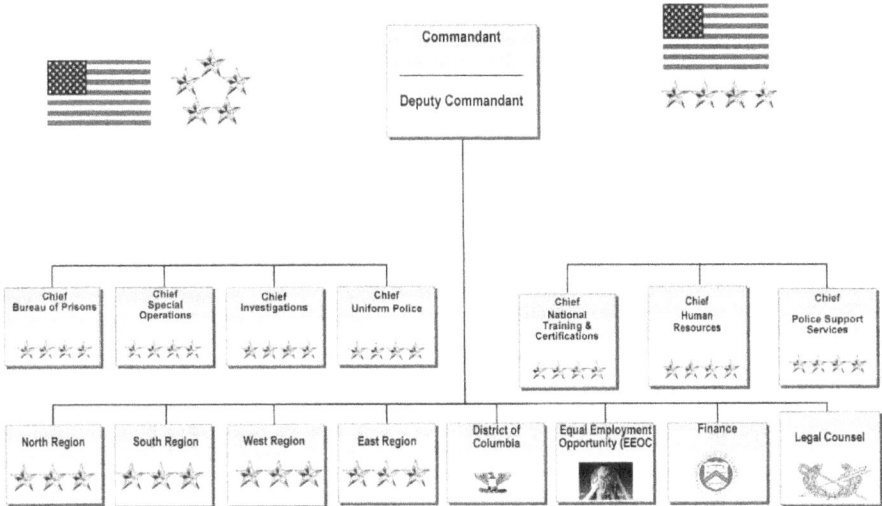

National Police Agency Core Mission Areas

- Serve and protect the people; maintain public order; coordinate, cooperate, support and respect the sovereignty of individual states and territories

- Carry out the day to day operations of the National Police Authority and provide police services for the 50 states and territories

- Investigate and conduct criminal investigations of federal, state, and select local laws and other applicable laws as defined in the National Police Act

- Executive Protection for the President, Vice President, and all branches of government as defined in the National Police Act and applicable laws

- Maintain and fully implement an effective Border Security, Customs Enforcement, and Immigrations and Naturalizations Service

- Traffic regulation on national highways, state, and local roadways

- International criminal investigation assistance

- Police training, certifications, credentialing, and development of national standards

Organizations Attached to the National Police Agency

NPA-attached organizations include the National Police Academy (Federal Law Enforcement Training Center – FLETC), the National Research Institute of Police Science and Technology, the Secret Service, and a host of agencies and organizations outlined in the National Police Act. The National Police Academy provides training to all police officers from all disciplines and carries out academic research.

As depicted in the (notional) National Police Act, experts in each department serve as instructors or researchers. Academy sub-units that provide advanced and expert training and conduct research include, the Highest Training Institute for Investigation Leaders, the Research and Training Center for International Criminal Investigation and Police Cooperation, the Police Policy Research Center, the Police Information-Communications Research Center, the Police Information-Communication Academy, and the Research and Training Center for Financial Crime Investigation.

The National Research Institute of Police Science conducts research in forensic science and applies the results in the examination and identification of evidence collected during police investigations. The agency also conducts juvenile crime prevention and traffic accident research. The Institute's seven departments are General Affairs; First, Second, Third and Fourth Forensic Science; Criminology and Behavioral Sciences; and Traffic. The Secret Service provides protection for the President, Vice President, and other designated officials per directives.

The National Police Organization headquarters office would be positioned in the National Capitol Region, Washington, DC. The Secretary, Deputy Secretary, Commissioners, Commandant, Deputy Commandant, and their staffs would be assigned to the headquarters office.

The national mission would be decentralized (full authority to manage and execute duties in respective region) into four major regions (North Region Chief Office in Minneapolis, Minnesota - East Region Chief Office in New York City, New York - South Region Chief Office in Dallas, Texas and West Region Chief Office in San Diego, California).

The regional offices would be supported by a fully staffed State Liaison Office. They would report directly to the respective Region Chief. The Region Chief serves primarily to work legal and legislative issues developing from enforcement of federal, state and local laws, courts, prison systems, and emergency coordination.

President of the United States of America

Secretary of the National Police
(Chairman National Public Safety Commission)

National Public Safety Commission

Commandant National Police Agency

G7

Bureau of Prisons   Special Operations   Investigations   Uniform Police

National Training   Human Resources   Police Support Services

(Notional Organizational Structure of National Police Model)

※

CHAPTER 7 - NATIONAL SUPPORT FOR A NEW DIRECTION

How effective would a National Police Agency be if implemented in the US?

San Diego County Sheriff William Gore

Sheriff William Gore

San Diego County (California) Sheriff William "Bill" Gore acknowledged support for establishing a National Police Agency in the U.S. According to Sheriff Gore, a national model could bring needed improvements within the criminal justice system.

Sheriff Gore is a former FBI Agent of 32 years. He served as Undersheriff before being appointed by the San Diego County Supervisors to interim Sheriff following the retirement of former Sheriff William B. Kolender. He was elected to his first term in the fall of 2010 and re-elected to his current term in the 2014 general elections.

Sheriff Gore supports the national model because it would eliminate existing barriers between federal and state officials, streamline budget and management processes, substantially reduce the number of officers, and support personnel needed to meet objectives. In addition, he supports the national model because it would develop needed national standards for sworn law enforcement officers.

Sheriff Gore believes that a large segment of local governments are experiencing extreme difficulties in paying salaries, acquiring new technology to combat high tech crimes, purchasing baseline equipment, and sustaining current infrastructures. Many local politicians would support this measure because it would relieve them of most financial problems inherent with maintaining public safety. He does not believe a debate on the issue would cause a stir within the law enforcement community. He also does not believe a nationalized police would be a "big pill" for most Americans to swallow.

According to Sheriff Gore, at some point in the future the federal government and a significant number of states will be forced into a compromise on some type of national or regional model to sustain police services. California is a prime example why a national model or an equivalent should be given serious consideration.

Former Jacksonville Sheriff Nathaniel Glover

Sheriff William Gore

Former Jacksonville (Florida) Sheriff Nathaniel Glover, Jr., does not support a National Police Agency in the U.S. Sheriff Glover is presently President of Edward Waters College, a nationally accredited college in Jacksonville, Florida and his alma mater. Sheriff Glover was elected to two terms as Sheriff of the Jacksonville Sheriff's Office (JSO) in 1995 and 1999. He was also the city's first African-American to be elected Sheriff in Florida since Reconstruction.

Sheriff Glover has enormous popularity in Jacksonville and throughout the law enforcement community. Of his many attributes, he is most impressive at handling crisis and controversial situations. He has an enviable ability to stay cool and make accurate decisions under enormous pressure.

In contrast to Sheriff Gore, Sheriff Glover does not support a National model. He believes the current model (local, state, tribal, and federal agencies working cooperatively), when compared to other agencies around the world is the best system. In some regards it closely resembles a National Police Force.

He concedes that a national model would bring about organizational and long term financial efficiencies. However, he does not believe a National Agency would have the local law enforcement accountable to the people, particularly in smaller communities.

The size of such an agency and the bureaucracy that would be created in order to carry out its mission would not allow it to be as sensitive to local community concerns. Also, it would not be as sensitive to civil liberties. He is not critical of the federal government and its ability to maintain law and order, but instead believes accountability for law enforcement is best held locally.

Police Chief Rosie Sizer

A recent case in Portland, Oregon highlights potential concerns expressed by Sheriff Glover in reference to local government's authority to self-govern. In May 2010, **Portland, Oregon's Chief of Police, Rosie Sizer,** was fired by **Mayor Sam Adams** two days after publicly blasting the mayor's proposed police budget. The mayor cited other issues and added that this demonstration of insubordination was the final straw.

Mayor Sam Adams n Chef Mike Reese

If Mayor Adams was not particularly pleased with the Regional Chief or District Chief under a national agency, where would he have taken his case for resolution? The National Police Act would require Public Safety Commissions to be established in each Region to resolve issues at the local and state levels. It is reasonable to assume these commissions would be a mix of state, local, federal officials, and ordinary citizens within the region.

The National Police Act would place limits on the number of commissions allowed in the region. It would also set criteria for membership similar to the National Public Safety Commission. Sheriff Glover's concerns are well noted regarding the inadvertent bureaucracy that such an enormous agency would create, making it difficult to resolve issues at low levels in a timely manner.

Former Oklahoma Governor Frank Keating

Governor Frank Keating

Governor Frank J. Keating was Oklahoma's governor when Timothy McVeigh parked a Ryder truck filled with explosives in front of the Alfred P. Murrah Federal building, setting off an explosion that claimed the lives of 168 people and seriously wounding hundreds more. He is a former FBI Agent and U.S. Attorney who has supervised several federal law enforcement agencies.

Governor Keating does not support a National Police Agency. However, he does believes the subject is worthy of national debate. Speaking from his Council of American Insurers office in Washington, DC, he is eager to join the debate on a National Police Agency. In the U.S., Governor Keating's experience in government and law enforcement is extensive and broad. He is widely considered to be the authority on government and law enforcement issues.

Although he considers himself more of a federalist (someone who believes in a strong and central government) regarding the issue of a national police agency, he believes the states should be given every opportunity to make, enforce, and prosecute criminal laws. According to Governor Keating, such an agency would not only violate the 10th amendment. It would be contrary to the goals, traditions, and fundamentals of America's democratic form of government.

Governor Keating believes an agency of such size and authority would be too large to manage. In particular, because of numerous challenges involving the Department of Homeland Security (DHS) and the Transportation Security Administration (TSA). A federal national police agency would be symbolic of "big government" and would have more regulations to enforce.

Governor Keating offered a regional police construct as an alternative to a national police within the states. Governor Keating cited numerous successful programs like one being used in San Diego County where incorporated cities (San Marcos, Vista, and Santee) contract out their police services to the Sheriff's Department.

Governor Keating said the current model (local, state, tribal and federal agencies working cooperatively) offers the best practice construct when compared to other international agencies. He believes cooperation and sharing information between the states and federal government is the right way for government to uphold its shared constitutional responsibilities.

Montana Governor Brian Schweitzer Response to Inquiry

Governor Brian Schweitzer

The strongest opposition to a National Police came from Montana Governor Brian Schweitzer. He believes this model would be perceived as an attempt by "Big Brother" to expand its control of state affairs. According to Governor Schweitzer, Montana citizens would fight to their last breath on any suggestion of a National Police. This is an agency they would clearly perceive to be tantamount to a government takeover.

A centrally managed and consolidated police force would bring needed efficiencies during times of a fragile economy. However, a compelling argument could be made against a National Police. Support of Montana's position on a central police authority is high throughout the U.S. Many private and public observers have a deep fear of losing local control over police and corrections functions.

Minneapolis Chief of Police Tim Dolan

Police Chief Tim Dolan

Chief Tim Dolan, Minneapolis (MN) Chief of Police, concedes there are efficiencies with a central agency. However, he does not envision a national agency in America. He welcomes a regional construct within the states and metropolitan areas. Chief Dolan does not believe the nation is ready for a federal government police program. Most people in his region are skeptical of the

U.S. government's openness and intervention into local issues. (Appendix A)

Maricopa County Sheriff Joseph Arpaio

Sheriff Joseph Arpaio

Sheriff Joe Arpaio of Maricopa County Sheriff's Office (AZ), does not support a National Police. He believes local law enforcement is best served in the communities and controlled by the local governments.

Inside major market cities and locales, consolidation and even a central government managed law enforcement program, is not beyond the realm of possibility. However, in most rural and small towns across the nation, many people like as little government intrusion in their lives as possible. Giving up local control of their police departments would be tantamount to surrendering part of their independence and identity to a distant governing body that would be oblivious to their needs, demands, and concerns.

"Under the constitution, there was never meant to be a Federal Police Force. Even a FBI limited only to investigations was not accepted until this century. The sacrifice of individual responsibility and the concept of local government by the majority of American citizens have permitted the army of bureaucrats to thrive. We have depended on government for so much for so long that we as people have become less vigilant of our liberties"
-US Representative Ron Paul, 1997

※

CHAPTER 8 - EXAMINATION OF FACTS FOR A NATIONAL POLICE AGENCY

"The powers not delegated to the United States by the Constitution, nor prohibited by it to the states, are reserved to the states respectively, or to the people."

Would a National Police Agency violate the 10th Amendment to the U.S. Constitution?

A national system operating as a central agency in the place of the current police structure would directly challenge the ideals of a government for the people, of the people, and by the people would be irrespective of potential economic advantages. The framers of the U.S. Constitution did not intend for the central government to usurp powers from the states, restricting their ability to make and enforce laws within their sovereignty.

Central Issues

Issue #1: Would the establishment of a NPO violate Article X of the United States (U.S.) Constitution? Would this creation interfere with sovereign power of individual states to make and enforce civil and criminal laws?

Issue #2: Why a national police? What evidence supports a constitutional amendment? In contrast, can America's deteriorating infrastructure and austere budgets across the 50 states continue to support over 17,000 police agencies?

Discussion on the 10th Amendment

There are essentially two ways spelled out in the Constitution on how to propose an amendment. One of which has never been used.

The first method is for a bill to pass both houses (Senate and House of Representatives) of the legislature, by a two-thirds majority in each. Once the bill has passed both houses, it goes on to the states. This is the route taken by all current amendments. There are some long outstanding amendments, such as the 27th amendment. Congress will normally put a time limit (typically seven years) for the bill to be approved as an amendment.

The second method is for a Constitutional Convention to be called by two-thirds of the legislatures of the States. That Convention would then propose one or more amendments. These amendments are sent to the states to be approved by three-fourths of the legislatures or conventions. This route has never been taken. There is discussion in political science circles on how such a convention would be convened and what kind of changes it would bring about.

Regardless of which of the two proposal routes is taken, the amendment must be ratified or approved by three-fourths of states. There are two ways to do this, also. The text of the amendment may specify whether the bill must be passed by the state legislatures or by a state convention. Amendments are sent to the legislatures of the states by default. Only one amendment, the 21st, specified a convention. In any case, passage by the legislature or convention is by simple majority.

- The Constitution, then, spells out four paths for an amendment:
- Proposal by convention of states, ratification by state conventions *(never used)*

- Proposal by convention of states, ratification by state legislatures *(never used)*

- Proposal by Congress, ratification by state conventions *(used once)*

- Proposal by Congress, ratification by state legislatures *(used all other times)*

The President does not have a role in the formal amendment process, though he would be free to make his opinion known. He cannot veto an amendment proposal and he cannot veto ratification. This point is clear in Article 5 and was reaffirmed by the Supreme Court in Hollingsworth v Virginia (3 US 378 [1798]). The President's power to veto applies only to the ordinary cases of legislation. He has nothing to do with the proposition or adoption of amendments to the Constitution.

"By law, a National Police would be unconstitutional, but it might be very practical. That is why we have a U.S. Department of Education (DOE) and U.S. Department of Health and Human Services (HHS). It is practical and easy to have such centralized control. That does not mean it is Constitutional however, and just because something is practical does not mean we (the people) should give up the protections of the Constitution for mere practicality." —**Ponzio Oliverio, JD**

Professor Ponzio Oliverio

Attorney Ponzio Oliverio

San Diego based Ponzio Oliverio, an Assistant Professor at National University Criminal Justice department and former Associate Attorney at Bobbitt, Pinckard & Fields A.P.C., was consulted on the constitutional interpretations of creating a National Police Agency in America. Professor Oliverio served 24 years as a Deputy Sheriff in San Diego County before retiring in 2010 to start a new career at Bobbitt, Pinckard, & Fields law firm. He is a seasoned and well-respected educator in the San Diego area Criminal Justice community.

Although Professor Oliverio does not support a National Police Agency in the U.S., he does concede that there are efficiencies and practicalities with such an agency. He believes that it would have support on both sides of the political aisles.

According to Professor Oliverio, the Constitution does not "create" or grant rights to the people, it merely enumerates or lists certain rights the people have just by virtue of being people. The ninth amendment was added to prevent an older rule of statutory interpretation, in Latin called, inclusio unius est exclusio alterius (the inclusion of one thing necessarily excludes all others).

According to the 10th amendment, unless the Constitution specifically gives the federal government some authority then it does not have the authority. This would indicate that because a National Police Force is not specifically included in the Constitution, it is therefore, not constitutional. Professor Oliverio explained that the federal government has demonstrated a pattern of repeated encroachments on the 10th amendment and has exceeded the scope of its authority on many occasions for many years. Examples would include many of the current federal agencies which do not have Constitutional authority to exist, yet they exist in abundance nonetheless.

Professor Oliverio cited many instances where the federal government created laws and agencies that should not be needed because there should not be very many federal crimes. Today, federal officials prosecute bank robberies, auto thefts, and a broad range of drug crimes which ordinarily should be under the purview of the states. The Constitution lists Congress' power in Article II section 8. Some of those powers would, by extrapolation, require enforcement so there could be some limited federal law enforcement agencies.

Congress controls naturalization so there can be an Immigration and Naturalization Service (INS). They control the Treasury which might require some form of policing to enforce counterfeiting laws. They also have authority over Post Offices, therefore, crimes relating to the Post Office could be enforced. However, outside of that the Constitution does not give authority for law enforcement.

Why do we have agencies such as the Federal Bureau of Investigations (FBI), Drug Enforcement Administration (DEA), and Bureau of Alcohol, Tobacco and Firearms (BATF)? Professor Oliverio noted that the Federal Bureau of Prisons (BOP) was not created until 1930 because there were few federal prisoners convicted exclusively of federal crimes. Inasmuch, at the time were few compared to the states. However, during the Franklin Delano Roosevelt (FDR) presidency, the scope and size of federal government grew exponentially. As evidenced by the recent health care legislation and financial bailouts, government has not stopped growing.

Professor Oliverio noted that our Constitution organically created the United States of America. In other words, the Constitution came first, then it created the government. Any document created by a legislative body can be changed by that same body. It takes much more than that to change our Constitution. Congress cannot, on its own, amend the Constitution.

Assistant District Attorney/ Prosecutor Cary T. Brown

Attorney Cary T. Brown

Cary T. Brown, Assistant District Attorney and Prosecutor, was consulted on the constitutional and law enforcement perspectives on a nationalized police in America. Cary has been a prosecutor for ten years in both Mississippi and Louisiana. He is a seasoned prosecutor and is well-respected within the law enforcement community.

Cary does not support nationalizing police forces. Nevertheless, he does offer meaningful insight on the subject. He stated, "Although I am not a supporter of a nationalized/centralized police force, I do believe the book raises some interesting issues."

He continued, "...it is my opinion that a Nationalized Police Force is in direct violation of the 10th Amendment to the United States Constitution. A plain reading of our Constitution reveals that the Framers did not delegate or reserve any authority to the Federal Government for the purpose of creating such a national agency. Assuming, arguendo that a Nationalized Police Force is constitutional; I am opposed to it for other practical reasons."

Tip O'Neill once said, "All politics are local." The same can be said of policing. From its inception, the foundation for localized policing has been built upon the trust and confidence that citizens have in their locally elected sheriff and police chief to protect their community and property. It is my belief that any Nationalized Police Force would have a difficult time obtaining the acceptance of the local communities that they are charged with policing, - thereby creating distrust and a lack of confidence in the ability of the police to protect its citizenry. This distrust can lead to vigilante justice and a breakdown of the very fabric of our laws.

As a prosecutor, there are certainly challenges in dealing with a variety of different police agencies throughout Louisiana. Each of these agencies has different funding mechanisms, resources, personnel, training and standards that are unique to that parish or municipality. Some of these smaller agencies do not have police officers that are P.O.S.T. certified and others simply cannot afford adequate training or equipment for their officers. Certainly, there are many flaws associated with our current system of policing, particularly as it relates to uniform training and standards.

However, I believe these issues are better addressed by the individual states and municipalities through legislative efforts and local elections. Simply put, the power should remain with the people, by and through the ballot box and their legislators. I would much rather work together with our local agencies to overcome issues and preserve the diversity of our people, culture, and communities than deal with the bureaucracy of another federal agency".

※

CHAPTER 9 - LAW ENFORCEMENT AGENCIES IN THE U.S ELIGIBLE FOR CONSOLIDATION

"Whoever, except in cases and under circumstances expressly authorized by the Constitution or Act of Congress, willfully uses any part of the Army or the Air Force as a posse comitatus or otherwise to execute the laws shall be fined under this title or imprisoned not more than two years, or both"

Title 18 USC § 1385. Use of Army and Air Force as posse com

The Posse Comitatus Act may prevent certain military intervention and enforcement of civil and criminal laws. For this reason, the Department of Defense (DoD) police agencies would be exempt from the consolidation and responsible only for DoD enforcement requirements.

Recognized Federal Law Enforcement Agencies

Agency	Department	Enforcement	Manpower	Budget
Coast Guard Police/ Investigative Service	Department of Homeland Security (DHS) U.S. Coast Guard	Maritime Security and Drug Interdiction	Act Duty- 42,000 Reserve - 7,500 Auxiliary- 29,000 Civilian - 7,700 Total: 86,200	$9,346,022,000
Customs and Border Protection Border Patrol	DHS (CBP)	Border Security	54,868	$10,941,231,000
Federal Protective Services	DHS (FPS)	Law Enforcement & Security of Federal Buildings & Leased Properties	2100	$615,000,000
Immigrations and Customs Enforcement	DHS (ICE)	Enforcement of Customs and Immigrations laws	20,546 (2011)	$5,676,085,000
Criminal Investigations & Uniform Police	DHS United States Secret Service	Executive Protection & Financial/Electronic Crimes	6,732	$1,639,346,000

Continue On Next Page

(CONTINUED) Recognized Federal Law Enforcement Agencies

Agency	Department	Enforcement	Manpower	Budget
Transportation Security Administration & Federal Air Marshal Service	DHS (TSA) (Air Marshals)	Protect the Transportation System	51,448	$7,101,828,000
Bureau of Alcohol, Tobacco, Firearms & Explosives	Department of Justice (DOJ) (BATF)	Enforcement of Firearms and Explosive laws	4,559	$1,120,000,000
Drug Enforcement Administration	DOJ (DEA)	Drug Enforcement and Interdiction	10,784	$2,415,000,000
Federal Bureau of Investigations	DOJ (FBI)	Federal Criminal Investigations, Counterterrorism	35,506	$7,900,000,000
Federal Bureau of Prisons	DOJ (BOP)	Federal Prisons	38,826	$523,200,000
United States Marshals Service	DOJ Federal Marshals	Protection of Federal Courts, Fugitive and Prisoner Transportation	9,708	$1,200,000,000
Diplomatic Security Service	Department of State (DOS) (DSS)	Diplomatic Security, Counterterrorism, Cyber Security	34,000	$2,845,000,000
Fisheries Office of Law Enforcement	Department of Commerce (DOC) National Oceanic and Atmospheric Administration	Ecosystem protection and conservation of most of national marine life	200+	$5,400,000
Criminal Investigations	Department of Treasury (IRS)	Investigates potential criminal violations of the U.S. Internal Revenue Code and related financial crimes	4400	$5,113,926
U.S. Mint Police	Treasury U.S. Mint	Protection for over $100 billion in Treasury and other government assets stored in U.S. Mint facilities	650	$46,624,000
Office of the Inspector General	Department of Education (DOE)	Identifying, auditing and investigating fraud, waste, abuse and mismanagement		
Office of Criminal Investigations	Department of Health and Human Services (FDA)	Enforcement of regulations and supervision of food safety, tobacco, prescription and over-the-counter pharmaceutical drugs	9,300	$2,300,000,000

Continue On Next Page

(CONTINUED) Recognized Federal Law Enforcement Agencies

Agency	Department	Enforcement	Manpower	Budget
Law Enforcement and Criminal Investigations / Inspector General	U.S. Department of Agriculture (USDA) U.S. Forest Service	Administers the nation's 155 national forests and 20 national grasslands	28,330	$5,086,000,000
Bureau of Indian Affairs Police Office of Justice Services	U.S. Department of Interior (DOI) Bureau of Indian Affairs	Law enforcement arm of the BIA -polices Indian tribes and oversee other tribal police organizations	683	$303,855,000
Office of Law Enforcement and Security	DOI Bureau of Land Management (BLM)	Protection of natural resources, employees and visitors	S Agents – 100 Rangers - 236	$27,957,000
U.S. National Park Service Rangers	DOI National Park Service	Protection and preservation of areas set aside in the National Park System		$2,261,559,000 (Total for National Park System)
U.S. Park Police	DOI National Park Service	Policing many of the famous monuments in the U.S. and all lands administered by the Service	600	See above for National Park System
Office of Law Enforcement	DOI U.S. Fish and Wildlife Service	Protects fish, wildlife and plant resources	295	$63,300,000
Federal Reserve Police	U.S. Federal Reserve System	Protection to Federal Reserve		
U.S. Capitol Police	U.S. Congress (Capitol Police)	Protection of U.S. Congress within the District of Columbia and throughout the United States and its territories	1800+	$376,020,000
Postal Inspectors Investigators Uniform Police	U.S. Postal Service	Investigate fraud against U.S. Mail, postal system or postal employees	4,000	
Supreme Court Police	U.S. Supreme Court	Protection of the Supreme Court building, the Justices, employees, guests and visitors	145	
Veterans Affairs Police	U.S. Department of Veterans (VA)	Protection of the VA Medical Centers and other facilities operated by U.S. VA	3200+	

Recognized Federal Law Enforcement Agencies

There are 26 state agencies identified as Highway Patrol and 23 agencies identified as State Police (some are commonly referred to as State Troopers). One state, Hawaii, does not have a state police agency. Instead, Hawaii has a Department of Public Safety (DPS). Some of the first State Police agencies were the Texas Rangers (1835), the Colorado Mounted Rangers (1861), the Pennsylvania (PA) Capitol Police (1895), and the Arizona Rangers (1901).

State agencies identified as Highway Patrols usually, but not always, limit their authority to patrolling state and federal highways. State Police agencies function much the same as local agencies but with statewide jurisdiction and state crime laboratories.

Thirty-five states have additional agencies with police or investigative powers. These "limited purpose" agencies have familiar acronyms like ABC (Alcohol Beverage Control), DCI (Department of Criminal Investigation), DMV (Department of Motor Vehicles), or SBI (State Bureau of Investigation). Where these agencies exist, they often share power with their state police counterparts under an umbrella organization such as a Department of Public Safety, a Department of Law Enforcement, or a State Department of Justice.

There are approximately 3,100 Sheriff's Departments in the U.S. Sheriffs are elected officials who exercise political control and influence within their jurisdiction. In most counties, the sheriff receives operating funds from the County Commissioners or the County Supervisors (like in San Diego County). The County Supervisors are also elected officials.

Some counties (like Orleans Parish in Louisiana) have two Sheriffs. One criminal and the other civil. Sheriffs, in general, have other duties in addition to law enforcement. This includes running a jail, collecting taxes, serving papers, and courthouse security. A contract system also exists where cities contract with the Sheriff's Office for police services. Such a model exists in San Diego County where some of the local cities (Santee, San Marcos) contract with the Sheriff for police services.

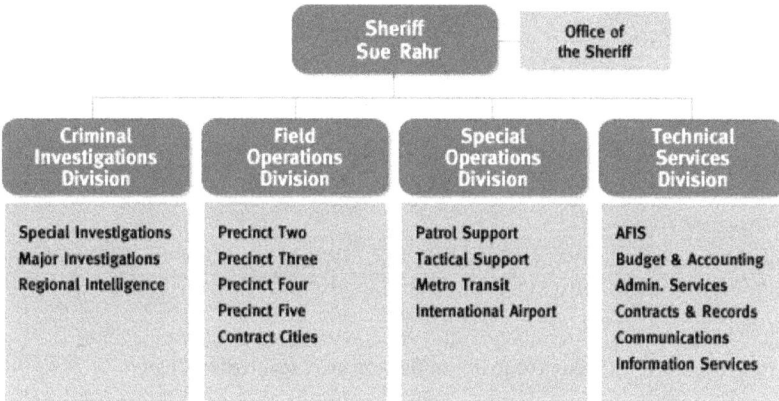

King County, WA Sheriff's Department Organization Chart

There are more municipal police departments (over 12,000) in the U.S. than any other kind of agency. This number includes transit, school, and housing police. There are about 800 departments that have only one officer. New York Police Department (NYPD), however, is in a class by itself with about 40,000 regular sworn officers (larger than the Canadian Army) and 13,000 special purpose transit, school, and housing officers.

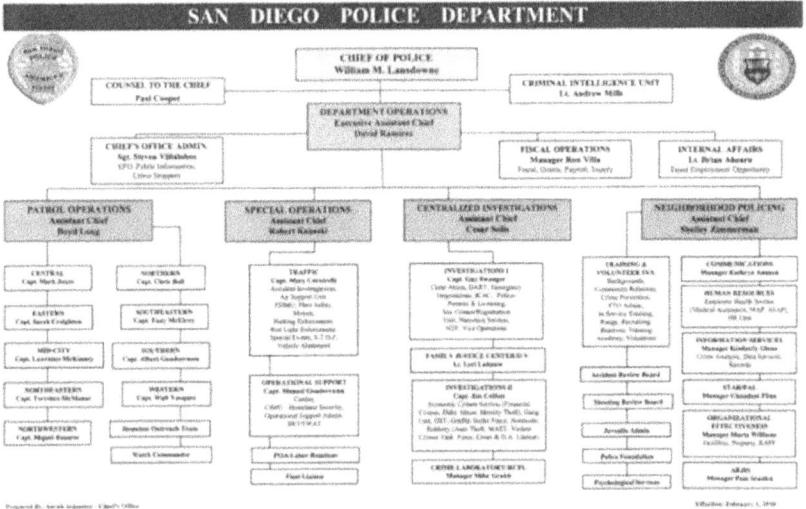

San Diego Police Department Organization Chart

Most municipal departments are small, having 10 officers or less. The large number of these "micro" agencies helps keep the average size of all police departments in America at around 25 sworn officers. Without counting civilians, this a measure of police strength. Counting civilians is a measure of professional growth.

"Macro" agencies with 1000 officers or more usually have specialized units, such as Crime Analysis and the Occasional Profiler Unit. "Medium" to "large" sized agencies with 26 to 999 (average 150) officers usually maintain extensive order maintenance functions assigned to municipal "peacekeeping" agencies.

Training to become a city or county police officer consists of attending a municipal police training academy which usually has an extensive curriculum for Basic Law Enforcement Training (BLET) to satisfy Peace Officers Standards and Training (POST) certification. In addition to the local police, more than 700 public and state colleges/universities employ campus law enforcement agencies. A majority of these public schools have sworn officers with arrest powers equivalent to their local counterparts in the city and county.

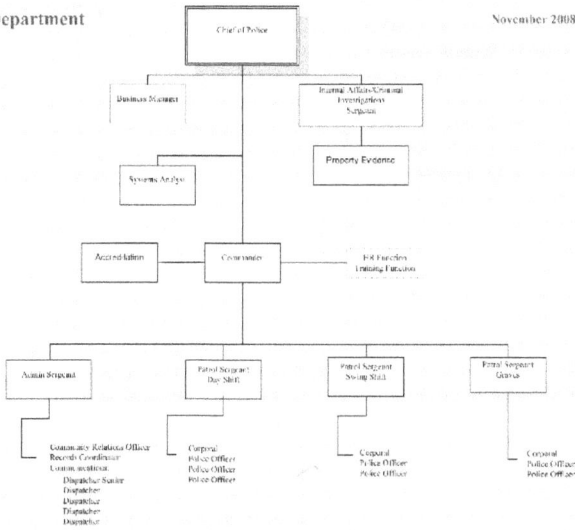

Northern Arizona University Police Department

According to the National Congress of American Indians (NCAI), police in Indian Country function within a complicated jurisdictional net, answer to multiple authorities, operate with limited resources, and patrol some of the most desolate of territory. This is often done without assistance from partner law enforcement agencies. There are only 2,380 Bureau of Indian Affairs and Tribal uniformed officers available to serve an estimated 1.4 million Indians.

This covers over 56 million acres of Tribal lands in the lower 48 states.

Among the most important challenges facing these officers and departments is providing around-the-clock police coverage to their communities. These departments rarely have more than one officer on duty at any time and their officers often work without adequate backup. They routinely work across numerous police and administrative functions. The challenge is to create workable, nation-specific policing institutions and approaches informed by traditional customs. They lay the best foundation for improving safety, preventing crime, and promoting the practice of effective policing in Indian Country.

※

CHAPTER 10 - CAN A CENTRAL POLICE AGENCY WORK IN THE U.S.?

Continued growth and unsure long term prospects will eventually force the governments to rethink how police services are managed and organized

Small and medium-sized police agencies are experiencing difficulties finding money to train their officers, acquire new and more sophisticated technology to prevent and combat crimes that are becoming more difficult to prosecute. They are also finding it more difficult to hire enough officers to meet the demands in their jurisdiction. Local politicians are confronted with deciding whether to hire new officers or purchase needed fire protection equipment for their Fire Departments. Continued growth and unsure long term prospects will eventually force the governments to rethink how police services are managed and organized to perform with less money to operate. Despite these challenges, most Americans would not support nationalizing police services even during austere economic conditions.

Many of the public officials contacted for this study were reluctant to go on record about a National Police Agency. San Diego County Sheriff Bill Gore said he would support a National Police Agency. Sheriff Gore is on the frontlines of the new age in crime fighting and he believes a paradigm change is needed in the way we approach law enforcement going forward into the 21st century. Minneapolis Police Chief Tim Dolan supports exploring options for Regional Police agencies within the states or more metropolitan departments.

Creation of a National Police Organization would be significantly different from consolidating a few federal agencies. Such a transformation would equate to a paradigm change. The agency would be among the largest and most complex police agency in the world with exclusive powers to enforce federal and state laws including local ordinances. The agency would have complete autonomy to protect the homeland, counter terror attacks or plots to the degree would-be terrorists would be discouraged from carrying out attacks on America's soil.

Regardless which direction is chosen, there will be critics of the plan. One such critic was the late Patrick Murphy a former New York Police Commissioner. Murphy once wrote that many communities are policed by a farcical little collection of untrained individuals who are really nothing more than guards. He implied that genuinely small departments (fewer than 25 sworn officers), to begin with, tend not to have much of a franchise by and large; with small territory and limited clientele, they do not face much of a crime problem.

Murphy was one of several reformers to suggest that these small police agencies should be eliminated or consolidated into larger and more professional departments. For example, one of the major recommendations made in 1967 by then President Lyndon Johnson's Commission on Law Enforcement and Administration of Justice was the coordination and consolidation of police services. Supporters of police consolidation tend to focus on two themes.

First, they claim that larger police organizations can make more efficient use of resources by taking advantage of the economies of scale resulting from eliminating redundant functions. Second, many believe that the fragmented nature of the American policing system results in poor communication, coordination and cooperation between police agencies. This results in an information-gap that allows victims and offenders to "slip between the cracks."Research by Elinor Ostrom and her colleagues casts at least some doubt on both of these concerns. They studied patterns of police service delivery in 80 mid-sized metropolitan areas throughout the U.S., containing 1,827 "police service producers." In a series of publications, Ostrom showed that when it comes to the size of a police organization, bigger is not necessarily better. Ostrom and other researchers have found that smaller police agencies often deliver more personalized services, have higher clearance rates and are able to deploy a higher proportion of their personnel "on the streets.

Ostrom also found that while metropolitan areas in the U.S. are policed by a patchwork of agencies, they have developed locally cooperative networks for delivering public safety across jurisdictional lines. These networks are joined together with an array of formal (contractual) and informal (handshake) agreements between agencies. Two techniques used to minimize the fragmentation are contracting services out between law enforcement agencies and forming mutual aid agreements that allow officers from neighboring agencies to render assistance as needed.

Cooperation also occurs among agencies at different levels of government. Many state police and highway patrol agencies provide patrol services on state roads, even when those roads traverse a community with its own police force. State and county agencies also routinely provide investigative assistance to smaller agencies, especially in the case of more serious offenses such as homicide or rape. The formality of these agreements ranges from verbal agreements to written legal contracts.

During the 1990s, there also was a proliferation of multijurisdictional "task forces" to combat rising violent crimes involving the illegal drug trade (drug-trafficking). According to one study, many were formed based on the realization that drug sellers did not respect jurisdictional boundaries. Law enforcement agencies serving contiguous jurisdictions therefore needed to coordinate enforcement activities both to share information and resources and to avoid overlapping investigations. These task forces often contain representatives from agencies at the city or town, county, state and/or federal levels.

The FBI allows state and local law enforcement agencies to access the National Crime Information Center (NCIC) database and the Automated Fingerprints Identification System (AFIS). It is also common practice for federal law enforcement agencies (such as the DEA and BATF), to be called into local and state jurisdictions to collaborate in solving certain offenses, especially those that cross jurisdictional boundaries.

Cooperation between agencies also exists at an international level. The International Criminal Police Organization (INTERPOL) enables law enforcement information to flow easily from officer to officer across borders, language barriers, time zones and terrains in the basic service of justice. INTERPOL was established in 1914 to respond to criminal activity that transcends international boundaries. Although INTERPOL is not an international police force and does not have police powers, it serves as a means of communication between law enforcement agencies across the world. INTERPOL membership consists of 176 countries.

Each member nation has a central headquarters called a National Central Bureau (NCB) that is managed by law enforcement officials from that country. The NCBs serve as hosts for information that is transmitted between INTERPOL members, as well as for information sent directly from INTERPOL's main headquarters, or the "General Secretariat," in Lyon, France. INTERPOL has been responsible for solving international crimes dealing with religious cult groups, drug-trafficking, art thefts, the child sex trade, computer software fraud, organized crime, counterfeit pharmaceuticals and money scams.

To foreign observers, the American system of policing seems disorganized and perhaps a bit chaotic. Despite the large number of agencies, a variety of mechanisms have been developed to seal the gaps between agencies. Thus, while law enforcement agencies at different levels of government do experience poor communication with other agencies and an occasional squabble over jurisdiction, they also cooperate with one another frequently.

The USA Patriot Act removed barriers within the federal government agencies that prevented information sharing. This authority expanded law enforcement powers to fight the war on terrorism. However, intelligence collection and criminally investigating crimes are two totally different programs and two different cultures. The cultures within the FBI and the Intelligence is quite different, e.g., prosecution versus information analysis.

Many experts would support a MI5 (British Domestic Intelligence Agency) model in the U.S. for domestic intelligence operations. This agency would be responsible for domestic intelligence gathering and intelligence operations within the U.S.

In Resolution

The American people have come to rely on the police for catching criminals, preventing crime, keeping the peace, maintaining order, interpreting the law, making people feel safe and secure in their homes and in a general sense, keeping things on an even keel. That is what the American people have come to expect from the Police.

An alternative to a central government police system is a consolidated or regional force structure to meet 21st century policing and protection issues. A collaborative effort between state and local governments should be strongly considered or encouraged to establish regional police forces. Regionalization and/or consolidation could dramatically reduce the current number of non-federal government police agencies across the nation.

A national system insofar as a central agency to replace the current police structure would directly challenge the ideals of a government for the people, of the people and by the people, irrespective of potential economic advantages. The framers of the U.S. Constitution did not intend for the central government to usurp powers from the states, restricting their ability to make and enforce laws within their sovereignty.

※

CHAPTER 11 - IN CLOSING

"Police have to be lawyers, scientists, medics, psychologists, athletes, and public servants."—**Ramsey Clark, former US Attorney General under President Lyndon B. Johnson 1967 – 1969**

Police, regardless if public or private, exist to do things that people generally do not want to do for themselves. Those of us who have worked in law enforcement for many years know the work is stressful, exciting, challenging, dangerous, and sometimes boring. Public service is the highest contribution one can do for their country. Police work is highly visible and the most scrutinized of any public position of trust.

A national police would cost the tax payers billions of dollars annually and there is no credible research identifying fiscal efficiencies. However, operational efficiencies and successes are foreseeable. At the end of the day, police exist to support the people in the local communities and the people should be allowed to hold the police accountable.

One could reasonably believe that to have a national police agency would bring about a more impartial approach and input, as well as, a greater objective analysis of any policing need. One could also assume that more adept attention to a policing concern and a consistency of mandates would serve to improve the efficacy of policing on the local, state, and national level. This would be the result of having a National Police Program.

Finally, one could further assume a national intervention would insist on a more regulated and consistent requirement (educationally) for officers preparing for the profession. A national intervention would require broader skill training in human relations and diversity among sworn police personnel on all levels.

Nevertheless, a national agency might offer some efficiencies. Such an agency would be difficult to manage. However, it would achieve successes in its core mission of the police primary responsibility to "protect and serve" the people.

"Accountability for the police is held locally and the people should keep this public responsibility."
- Former Jacksonville Sheriff Nathaniel Glover

※

AUTHOR PROFILE

Retired U. S. Navy Lieutenant Commander Curtis Page, Jr.'s experience as an Advisor and Subject Matter Expert for Military Police Operations, Navy Security and Force Protection at Battelle Memorial Institute coupled with his service in two civilian police agencies: Millington Police Department (Millington, Tennessee) and Kitsap County Sheriff's Office (Bremerton, Washington) have given him a unique hands on view of law enforcement in the United States.

In light of recent national media coverage of police conflicts, Lieutenant Commander Page's 25+ years of law enforcement experience and his training that includes an Associate of Arts degree, Bachelors of Science degree in Criminal Justice Administration and a Master's degree in Business Organizational Security Management have compelled him to author the book *A National Police in America "Is it Time for Change?"*

※

BIBLIOGRAPHY

Advisory Commission on Intergovernmental Relations (ACIR), "Metropolitan Organization: The Allegheny County Case," Washington, D.C., February 1992

Austin Peay University – 2010: U. S. Policy Agencies Structure and Organization - STATE- BY-STATE GUIDE to Federal Agencies, State/County/Municipal – Retrieved June 7, 2010
http://www.apsu.edu/oconnort/polstruct.htm

Bish, Robert L. "Local Government Amalgamations: Discredited Nineteenth-Century Ideals Alive in the Twenty-First," C.D. Howe Institute Commentary 150, March 2001

Black Rage in New Orleans: *Police Brutality and African American Activism from World War II to Hurricane Katrina* by Leonard Moore (Louisiana State University Press, 2010); "Shielded From Justice: Police Brutality and Accountability in the United States" (Human Rights Watch, 1998); History of New Orleans Police Department (City of New Orleans).

California Legislative Analyst's Office – November 18, 2009: California's Nonpartisan Fiscal And Policy Advisor - Retrieved on August 16, 2010
http://www.lao.ca.gov/2009/bud/fiscal_outlook/fiscal_outl ook_111809.aspx

Canada FAQ (2011) – Canada Questions and Answers: Everything You Need to Know About Canada
http://www.canadafaq.ca/what+type+of+government+does +canada+have/

Canada Ministry of Public Safety (2011) -
http://www.publicsafety.gc.ca/abt/wwa/index-eng.aspx
City of San Diego, California: 2007 After-Action Report – City of San Diego Response
Retrieved March 21, 2010
http://www.sandiego.gov/mayor/pdf/fireafteraction.pdf

City of San Diego, California Police:
http://www.sandiego.gov/police/

Commander, Navy Installations Command (CNIC), 2010:
http://www.cnic.navy.mil/CNIC_+HQ_Site/index.htm

Cornell University School of Law (2010) – U.S. Constitution
Bill of Rights: Retrieved on July 21, 2010
http://topics.law.cornell.edu/constitution/billofrights#amen
dmentx

Country Data (1996) - RUSSIA - A Country Study
http://www.country-data.com/frd/cs/rutoc.html#ru0213
March 1, 2011

County of San Diego, California: 2007 San Diego County
Firestorms After-Action Report
Prepared by E G & G Technical Services, Inc. February 2008
– Retrieved March 21, 2010
http://www.sdcounty.ca.gov/oes/docs/2007_SanDiego_Fire
_AAR_Main_Document_FINAL.pdf

 County of San Diego, California: 2010 Multi-Jurisdiction
Hazard Mitigation Plan (draft)
- Retrieved March 21, 2010
http://www.co.san-
diego.ca.us/oes/emergency_management/oes_jl_mitplan.ht
ml

County of San Diego, California: The San Diego Local Agency
Formation Commission
(LAFCO): Micro Report on Reorganization of Structural Fire
Protection and
Emergency Medical Services in Unincorporated San Diego
County – Retrieved March 22, 2010
http://www.sdlafco.org/mainpages/reportspublications.htm

County of San Diego, California Sheriff:
http://www.sdsheriff.net/

Enchanted Learning (2010) – The United States of America
Population and Demographics

Retrieved September 9, 2010
http://www.enchantedlearning.com/usa/statesbw/usa.shtml

Federalists – Early years of the American Government (2010)
Retrieved September 6, 2010
http://www.britannica.com/EBchecked/topic/203519/Feder
alist-Party

Feinstein, Diane (2011) – United States Senator, Washington,
DC 20510-0504 Letter dated
March 14, 2011 (California)

Haddow, G., Bullock, J. and Coppola, D. (2008) –
Introduction to Emergency
Management Third Edition, Publisher: Butterworth
Heinemann)
City of San Diego, California: After Action Report - October
2007 Wildfires, City of San Diego Response – Released on
March 6, 2008 – Retrieved March 21, 2010
http://www.sandiego.gov/mayor/pdf/fireafteraction.pdf

Jacksonville, Florida Sheriff:
http://www.coj.net/Departments/Sheriffs+Office/Default.ht
m

Law Library - American Law and Legal Information (2010)
Police – Organization and Management – Retrieved August
31, 2010 http://law.jrank.org/pages/1668/Police-
Organization-Management-American-system-policing.html

Las Vegas Metropolitan Police Department (2011) – History
of Law Enforcement Consolidation within Clark County,
Nevada – Retrieved February 1, 2011
http://www.lvmpd.com/about/consolidation.html

Library of Congress (1996), United States Congress - Country
Data (1996) - **RUSSIA - A Country Study**
http://www.country-data.com/frd/cs/rutoc.html#ru0213
March 1, 2011

Library of Congress (2011), United States Congress –
http://www.loc.gov/lawweb/servlet/lloc_news?disp3_2509_
text The Library of Congress

(2011) Russia Police of Law March 1, 2011 – Russian Federation: New Law on Police

London, Rick (2010) – Ezine Articles: A Brief History of Police in America – Retrieved

June 23, 2010 http://ezinearticles.com/?A-Brief-History-Of-Police-In-America&id=1179717

National Congress of American Indians (2010): The American Indian Country – Retrieved July 23, 2010 http://www.ncai.org/

Naval Post Graduate School (2007): The Journal of the Naval Post Graduate School Center for Homeland Defense and Security – Homeland Security Matters - Domestic Intelligence Agency for the United States - A Comparative Analysis of Domestic Intelligence Agencies and Their Implications for Homeland Security by James Burch – Retrieved August 24, 2010 http://www.hsaj.org/?fullarticle=3.2.2

New Yorker (2010) – Borderlines by William Finnegan on July 26, 2010 - Retrieved September 22, 2010 http://www.newyorker.com/talk/comment/2010/07/26/100726taco_talk_finnegan#ixzz10IJCg5p1

Oregonian Live (2010): Oregonianlive.com News story, *Sam Adams fires police Chief Rosie Sizer, names Mike Reese to the job,* published May 12, 2010. Retrieved on August 22, 2010 http://www.oregonlive.com/portland/index.ssf/2010/05/sam_adams_calls_noon_news_conf.html

Organization for Security and Cooperation in Europe (OSCE, 2011) – Policing Profiles of Participating and Partner States (Italy) http://polis.osce.org/countries/details?item_id=23 March 3, 2011

PEW Center (2010) PEW Center on the States – Issue Brief on Prison Count and the Costs of Maintaining Correctional Facilities - March 14, 2011 http://www.pewcenteronthestates.org/uploadedFiles/Prison_Count_2010.pdf

Priest, Dana and Arkin, William (2010) 1- The Washington Post report 19 July 2010:
Top Secret America - A Washington Post Investigation:
Retrieved on July 19, 2010
http://projects.washingtonpost.com/top-secret-america/

ProPublica (2014): *Deadly Force, in Black and White*. A ProPublica analysis of killings by police shows outsize risk for young black males by Ryan Gabrielson, Ryann Grochowski Jones and Eric Sagara ProPublica, Oct. 10, 2014, 10:07 a.m. Retrieved on December 23, 2014
http://www.propublica.org/article/deadly-force-in-black-and-white

Royal Canadian Mounted Police (2011) http://www.rcmp-grc.gc.ca/index-eng.htm

Slade, G. (2010) Open Democracy – International Security Relations Network (ISN) – Russia:
Crisis, Crime and Police Reform – March 1, 2011
http://www.isn.ethz.ch/isn/Current-Affairs/ISN-insights/Detail?lng=en&id=124461&contextid734=124461&contextid735=124460&tabid=124460

State of California: California Fire Siege 2007 Report & Southern California Wildfires
After Action/Corrective Action Report of July 2008 –
Retrieved on March 21, 2010
http://www.oes.ca.gov/WebPage/oeswebsite.nsf/699b301869389a02882573c900817d70/22933e652ad231b7882574100066cece/$FILE/2007%20SoCal%20Fires%20AAR%20Final%20Exec%20Sum_%20Report%2002_03_09.pdf

Tully, Edward J. (2002) - National Executive Institute Associates, Major Cities Chiefs
Associations, and Major County Sheriff's Association
January 2002 – Retrieved on June
15, 2010 from website
http://www.neiassociates.org/regionalization.htm

University of North Florida (2008) - Guide to the Jacksonville, Florida, government consolidation collection, *University of North Florida/Thomas G. Carpenter Library -*

Retrieved November 23, 2010
http://www.unf.edu/library/sc/jacksonvilleconsolidation.ht
ml

University of Albany (2007) – Local Government Case Study
– Waterford Police Department Dissolution, An
Intergovernmental Studies Program Case Study – University
of Albany – Rockefeller College of Public Affairs & Policy
United States Department of Homeland Security (DHS) –
Federal Emergency Management
Agency (FEMA) Federal Response to the California Wildfires
(2007) – Retrieved March 21, 2010
http://www.fema.gov/about/regions/regionix/ca_fires.shtm

United States Department of Justice – Bureau of Justice
Statistics (2010) – Total Correctional Population – Retrieved
on September 9, 2010
http://bjs.ojp.usdoj.gov/index.cfm?ty=tp&tid=11

United States Department of Justice – National Institute of
Justice (NIJ) 2010 – The President's Commission on Law
Enforcement and Administration of Justice (1967) –
Retrieved
September 2, 2010
http://www.ojp.usdoj.gov/nij/journals/257/40th-crime-
report.html

United States Department of Justice, Federal Bureau of
Investigations (2010): Uniform Crime
Reporting Program – Violent Crimes in the United States for
Calendar Year 2009 - Retrieved September 18, 2010
http://www.fbi.gov/ucr/cius2009/offenses/violent_crime/in
dex.html

United States Department of Justice (2011) Office of Justice
Programs - Bureau of Justice Assistance
http://www.ncjrs.gov/pdffiles1/bja/181249.pdf

United States Department of Justice, Office of Justice
Programs – Bureau of Justice Statistics:
Capital Punishment in the United States, 2013 – Retrieved
December 21, 2014
http://www.bjs.gov/index.cfm?ty=pbdetail&iid=5156

United States Department of Labor (2010) – Bureau of Labor Statistics: Occupational Outlook

Handbook, 2010 -11 Edition Retrieved November 24, 2011 http://www.bls.gov/oco/ocos160.htm

United States Department of Labor (2010) – Bureau of Labor Statistics: Retrieved
July 24, 2010 http://www.bls.gov/oco/pdf/ocos160.pdf 24 July 2010

United States Department of State (2011) – Profile of the Russian Federation
http://www.state.gov/r/pa/ei/bgn/3183.htm March 2, 2011

United States Department of State (2011) – Profile of Italy
http://www.state.gov/r/pa/ei/bgn/4033.htm March 2, 2011

United States of America - Location and size, Population, Manufacturing and construction, Energy and mining, Information technology
http://www.nationsencyclopedia.com/economies/Americas/United-States-of-America.html#ixzz0z69tuf5i

University of Alaska (2011) – University of Alaska Anchorage: Canadian Law Enforcement
http://justice.uaa.alaska.edu/rlinks/canada/lawenf.html

USA Today (August 15, 2014: Police Killings by Brad Heath, Kevin Johnson and Meghan Hoyer. Retrieved on December 23, 2014
http://www.usatoday.com/story/news/nation/2014/08/14/police-killings-data/14060357/

Wall Street Journal (2010): Lights Out at the Penitentiary – Strapped States is Shutting Prisons, But moving 1,100 inmates, Beds and All by Gary Fields – Retrieved September 6, 2010
http://online.wsj.com/article/SB125149123499467721.html

※

APPENDIX A

A National Police in America
"Is it Time for Change?"

(Copies of original letters written to Curtis Page, Jr.)

1.0 – Sheriff Joe Arpaio

Maricopa County Sheriff's Office

Joe Arpaio
Sheriff

Ph: 602-876-1801
Fax: 602-251-3877
Switchboard: 602-876-1000
www.mcso.org

100 West Washington, Suite 1900
Phoenix, AZ 85003

August 5, 2011

Mr. Curtis B. Page, Jr.
10325 Lake Ridge CT
Spring Valley, California 91977

Dear Mr. Page:

I apologize for my delayed response. Thank you very much for your note of February 17, 2011, and commending my staff and I on the way we operate the Maricopa County Sheriff's Office. It does mean a lot to me to know that you are "in my corner."

As Sheriff of Maricopa County, I do not support a National Police Agency.

Wishing you the best in the days to come, I remain,

Sincerely,

Joseph M. Arpaio
Sheriff

2.0 – Sheriff Bob Buckley, July 12, 2010

BOB BUCKLEY, SHERIFF
EX OFFICIO TAX COLLECTOR
100 East Bayou Street, Suite 101
Farmerville, LA 71241-2843

Office (318) 368-3124
Civil Division (318) 368-2510
Fax (318) 368-2728

July 12, 2010

Honorable Curtis B. Page, Jr., Commander (Retired)
10325 Lake Ridge Court
Spring Valle, CA 91977

Dear Mr. Page:

First of all, it is good to hear from one of my fellow Union Parish sons. Your accomplishments are outstanding.

Secondly, you ask how America migrated from only small city police organizations to the number we have today. It is my opinion and history may bear this out that America was founded and developed from people from all over the world with their main priority being freedom. Most, if not all, had been oppressed in one way or another by either a dictator or strong federalist form of government and they migrated to the new world for the freedom to choose and control the amount of "self government" they desired. They also wanted to control the amount of taxes paid and the services they desired. The idea of a police force was never envisioned until the concept of true community policing had been outgrown by the amount of lawlessness that grew in their communities, especially on the frontier.

The community policed itself first as you and I growing up. We could never do anything without our neighbors reporting us to our parents or the neighbors themselves applying the "peach tree limb". Even as we moved west, the concept of local law enforcement was much more accepted than the federal intervention thru either the deputy vs. marshals or the army that has continued to this day. We have the F.B.I., D.E.A., Customs-Border Patrol and other federal agencies, vested with police powers, but yet the people of Arizona passed a state law so that local authorities could handle the overwhelming problem of illegal immigration because the local people felt that the federal agencies could not or would not do their duty. Not only is this feeling shared in Arizona but in all the border states.

I firmly believe that the feelings of distrust brought over from Europe and Asia centuries ago in regard to controlling central government is just as strong today as it was then. People, especially in the majority of law enforcement agencies jurisdictions, most being less than 30 person departments, want to know their officers and want the officers to enforce the law as to the standard demanded by these same citizens.

Exhibit (Bo)

As a law enforcement officer in a small jurisdiction and as a retired state police trooper, I realize that the citizens are my boss and as such I must be available 24-7 to meet with them, take their phone calls and do their wishes within the perimeters of the law. I have to stand for election every four years and answer for my actions or inactions. In my humble opinion, I feel that there would be an uprising from the citizens if our local law enforcement was taken away and replaced with a federal force. I know that when the Farmerville and Marion Town Councils attempted to change the elected chief of police to an appointed one, they caught "pure Hell". Most of the councilmen had a tough time being re-elected.

I hope this has answered your questions with the exception of one. Would I support a national force? The answer would be no, not because of any animosity, but because this is not what my bosses would want.

As your sheriff, I am available to answer any questions you may have.

Respectfully,

Bob Buckley
Sheriff of Union Parish

3.0 – Police Chief Timothy Dolan, June 29, 2010

Minneapolis
City of Lakes

Police Department

Timothy J. Dolan
Chief of Police

350 South 5th Street - Room 130
Minneapolis MN 55415-1389

Office 612-673-2853
TTY 612-673-2157

June 29, 2010

Curtis B. Page, Jr
Senior Protection Advisor
Maritime Readiness and Protection
Battelle San Diego Operations
655 West Broadway
Suite 1420
San Diego, California 92101

Dear Curtis B. Page, Jr

You ask an interesting question. I do think that there are huge efficiencies, and very likely effectiveness benefits, with consolidating law enforcement. I would like to see more "metro" police departments in places like the Minneapolis/St.Paul area. A statewide police department also has huge efficiencies and likely effectiveness benefits. Taking city police off of city budgets would also be beneficial.

What you will run into, as far as resistance, is a general reluctance to give up city policing. There are many in the United States who fear giving up local control of their police. They may fear "big brother" or they may just like having some say in how their cities are policed. We see that already in their attitudes towards State Patrol and the State Park Rangers.

Moving to a metro concept - like Boston and Vegas PD's would be great. Statewide would make total sense in some state's with lower populations. I think it would take something really catastrophic to bring around a major change like national policing in the United States - like a major depression or a huge failure in domestic security. If cities could no longer afford police - like Detroit - nation wide, there would have to be change. If the American people lost faith in their local police being able to protect them from terrorism, there would have to be change.

Good luck with your course of study.

Sincerely,

Timothy J. Dolan, Chief

311

City Information
and Services

TJD/mr
www.ci.minneapolis.mn.us
Affirmative Action Employer

Exhibit (_B1_)

4.0 – Senator Dianne Feinstein

DIANNE FEINSTEIN
CALIFORNIA

SELECT COMMITTEE ON
INTELLIGENCE—CHAIRMAN
COMMITTEE ON APPROPRIATIONS
COMMITTEE ON THE JUDICIARY
COMMITTEE ON RULES AND
ADMINISTRATION

United States Senate

WASHINGTON, DC 20510–0504

http://feinstein.senate.gov

March 14, 2011

Mr. Curtis Page
10325 Lake Ridge Court
Spring Valley, CA 91977

Dear Mr. Page:

Thank you for writing to inquire about the history of law enforcement and the potential for a national police force. I appreciate your many years of service in the United States Navy Military Police Corps and local law enforcement. I also apologize for the delay in my response. For security reasons, postal mail is routed to an off-site facility for testing before it is released to my office, which delays the delivery process.

Efforts to prevent and address domestic crime have traditionally been the responsibility of state and local governments, with the federal government playing a supportive role. As crime rates increased throughout the 1960s, 1970s, and 1980s, the federal government became increasingly involved in anti-crime efforts. This was accomplished primarily through grant programs to encourage and assist states and communities in their efforts to control crime, and through expanding the number of offenses that could be prosecuted in federal courts.

I appreciate hearing your interest and research regarding the creation of a national police force in the United States. Please note that many federal agencies already have a strong law enforcement focus, including the Federal Bureau of Investigation, U.S. Marshals Service, and U.S. Secret Service. I would encourage you to conduct additional research on federal law enforcement agencies. There are resources on that subject at the Department of Justice website at http://www.justice.gov. As you recognize, completely replacing state and local law enforcement would be very controversial. To date, no legislation to do this has been introduced. Rest assured that, should such legislation be introduced, I will keep your views in mind.

Once again, thank you for writing. I hope you will continue to keep me informed on issues of importance to you. If you have any additional questions or concerns, please do not hesitate to contact my Washington, D.C. office at (202) 224-3841, or visit my website at http://feinstein.senate.gov.

Sincerely yours,

Dianne Feinstein
United States Senator

DF:to:jg

5.0 – Congressman Duncan Hunter

From: Congressman Duncan Hunter [CA52DHima@mail.house.gov]
Sent: Friday, July 09, 2010 12:53 PM
To: cbpagejr@att.net
Subject: Reply from Congressman Duncan Hunter

DUNCAN HUNTER
52ND DISTRICT, CALIFORNIA

COMMITTEE ON ARMED SERVICES

COMMITTEE ON
EDUCATION AND LABOR

U.S. House of Representatives
Washington, DC 20515–0552

July 9, 2010

Mr. Curtis B. Page
10325 Lake Ridge Ct
Spring Valley, CA 91977-5426

Dear Curtis:

Thank you for contacting me about my position on creating a national police organization. I welcome the opportunity to respond to you on this issue.

As you know from your own experience, local and state law police agencies have general enforcement duties that, in most cases, are different from the role and responsibility of federal law enforcement. At the state and local level, police officers do everything from patrolling communities to enforcing traffic laws. Federal law enforcement, such as the Federal Bureau of Investigation, is responsible for investigating violations of more than 200 categories of federal law and conducting national security investigations.

Given these defined duties and unique responsibilities, it is important that we strengthen the relationship between local, state and federal law enforcement without creating unnecessary interference among each of these entities. Adding a national police organization to the list of existing law enforcement agencies nationwide would likely serve to disrupt this relationship, redirect available resources and likely impact the availability of federal funding for existing law enforcement challenges. Also, consistent with the point raised in your letter, such an organization raises constitutional concerns under the 10th amendment and the rights granted to states.

I hope this answers your question. If you should need additional information, please don't hesitate to let me know.

Sincerely,

1

Exhibit (63)

Duncan Hunter
Member of Congress

Please visit my website at hunter.house.gov to sign up for my e-newsletter and receive electronic updates.

6.0 – Kim Lowry, August 16, 2010

U.S. Department of Justice

Office of Justice Programs

Office of Communications

Washington, D.C. 20531

AUG 1 6 2010

Curtis B. Page, Jr.
10325 Lake Ridge Court
Spring Valley, CA 91977

Dear Mr. Page:

Thank you for your letter to Attorney General Eric H. Holder, Jr., regarding assistance with your thesis project about the creation of a national police organization. Your letter was forwarded to the Department of Justice's Office of Justice Programs' (OJP) Office of Communications for a response.

We appreciate your interest in the prevention of crime and protection of our Nation. The Federal Bureau of Investigation, the United States Marshals Service, the Bureau of Alcohol, Tobacco, Firearms and Explosives, the Drug Enforcement Administration, and the Federal Bureau of Prisons are law enforcement agencies within the Department of Justice. Additionally, other federal law enforcement agencies including the United States Secret Service, the United States Immigration and Customs Enforcement, and the United States Customs and Border Protection play vital roles in service to the government and citizens of the United States. We are proud of the work that the men and women of these agencies do to help make America safer.

For more information, please visit the Department of Justice's website at www.usdoj.gov, or the Department of Homeland Security website at www.dhs.gov.

Sincerely,

Kim M. Lowry
Director

7.0 – FBI Special Agent Keith Slotter, June 25, 2010

U.S. Department of Justice

Federal Bureau of Investigation

In Reply, Please Refer to
File No.

June 25, 2010

Mr. Curtis B. Page, Jr.
Senior Protection Advisor
Maritime Readiness and Protection
Battelle San Diego Operations
655 West Broadway, Suite 1420
San Diego, CA 92101

Dear Mr. Page:

I am in receipt of your letter dated June 18, 2010 regarding your research project in conjunction with your pursuit of a Masters Degree in Business Organizational Security Management.

Per your request seeking an opinion on the viability of a National Police Organization in the United States given current conditions in this country, I would offer the following:

Throughout the history of the United States, the idea of establishing a National Police Force of some sort has been discussed and seriously considered at various times, particularly during the gangster era of the 1930s. Because of rampant gangsterism throughout the Midwest, Congress seriously considered establishing a National Police Force at that time, assuming the FBI would greatly expand and naturally assume that role. To his great credit, Director J. Edgar Hoover was adamantly opposed to the creation of such a national operation and truly believed that the war on crime was best fought by state and local police departments throughout the country with federal assistance from agencies like the FBI as needed and pursuant to existing federal laws. Since that time, the FBI's jurisdiction has expanded greatly with responsibility for over 300 federal violations. However, I believe that Director Hoover's vision for effective police cooperation in addressing all types of crimes was the correct one. Today the FBI, other federal agencies, and our state, local, and tribal partners participate in more task forces than ever before, including terrorism, violent crime, gang, mortgage fraud, public corruption and a variety of other matters. This unique cooperative effort in the U.S. is what has made our country's law enforcement presence so capable and strong. In my opinion, the creation of a National Police Force would weaken

Exhibit (A, 7)

rather than strengthen our current law enforcement and intelligence gathering capabilities. And while our current system is not perfect, we can take great pride in the men and women across the nation who put their lives on the line every day.

I hope this assists with your research project and wish you the very best in the future.

Sincerely,

Keith Slotter
Special Agent in Charge

APPENDIX B

A National Police in America
"Is it Time for Change?"

(Personal Interviews conducted by Curtis Page, Jr. and used as resource material.)

INTERVIEWS

Gore, W. D. (2010, July 1). San Diego County Sheriff. (J. Curtis B. Page, Interviewer)
Telephone conversation on issues involving establishment of a National Police Agency

Keating, F. (2010, July 6). Former Oklahoma Governor. (J. Curtis B. Page, Interviewer)
Telephone conversation on issues involving establishment of a National Police Agency

Nathaniel Glover, J. (2010, July 5). Former Jacksonville Sheriff. (J. Curtis B. Page, Interviewer)
Telephone conversation on issues involving establishment of a National Police Agency

Oliverio, P. (2010, July 7). San Diego based Attorney. (J. Curtis B. Page, Interviewer)
National University, University of Phoenix and former Associate Attorney, Bobbitt, Pinckard & Fields Law Firm on the constitutional issues involving creation of a National Police Agency

Random Field Interviews (2010-14, June 5). (J. Curtis B. Page,   Interviewer)
University of California (San Diego), San Diego State University, Grossmont College, Coleman University, Southwestern University, University of Phoenix, San Diego City College, Thomas Jefferson School of Law, University of San Diego, ITT Technical Institute, National University and San Diego Mesa College.

※

www.ingramcontent.com/pod-product-compliance
Lightning Source LLC
Chambersburg PA
CBHW060025210326
41520CB00009B/1001